T0354656

THE
CASE
FOR
HOPE

What I Learned on My Journey from
Cancer to Wellness: We Can Heal

JENNIFER LAGUZZA DICKENSON

BALBOA.PRESS
A DIVISION OF HAY HOUSE

Balboa Press books may be ordered through booksellers or by contacting:

Balboa Press
A Division of Hay House
1663 Liberty Drive
Bloomington, IN 47403
www.balboapress.com
844-682-1282

Print information available on the last page.

Library of Congress Control Number: 2022902080

ISBN: 978-1-9822-7946-2 (sc)
ISBN: 978-1-9822-7948-6 (hc)
ISBN: 978-1-9822-7947-9 (e)

Balboa Press rev. date: 06/13/2022

Disclaimer

The information herein is not intended to offer medical advice. The content of this book is for informational purposes only. The content is not intended to be, nor is it, a substitute for professional medical advice, diagnosis, or treatment. Author and her affiliates, successors, and assigns make no representations or warranties and expressly disclaim any and all liability concerning any treatment or action by any person following the information offered or provided within. You are advised to consult with your physician/health-care professional with regard to matters relating to your health and in particular regarding matters that may require diagnosis or medical attention. Never disregard professional medical advice or delay in seeking it because of something you have read in this book. If you choose to rely on information in this book for medical purposes, you do so at your own risk, and the author assumes no responsibility for your actions.

To my wonderful husband and daughters
and those curious about healing.

Contents

Introduction

The Case for Hope was born of necessity. When I was diagnosed with brain cancer (glioblastoma) in 2011, my world stopped. According to my doctors and the statistics, I would not survive it. Of course, it was devastating, but after some time, I started to consider something else: hope. Hope that I could beat it and live a healthy life again. Hope that I could discover how I got in this situation in the first place and learn from it.

With those ideas in mind, I asked myself two basic questions:

1. *If just one person can beat this disease, why can't I?*
2. *Since we naturally heal ourselves all the time with cuts, colds, and broken bones, why can't I heal this, too?*

These questions created hope in me. And although hope is not a strategy in and of itself, it can be the spark that creates action, and action can create change. In the case of illness, change can occur when we learn about and use healing tools and find balance and wellness in our lives.

By being curious and feeling compelled to find a way to beat my abysmal diagnosis, even with the traditional medical treatment I was going to receive, I began to learn about the many facets of healing through the mind, body, and spirit. One discovery would lead to another and another, like alchemy. In this way, I stepped into a mystery that changed my entire life.

Among other things, I was learning that healing isn't just about surgeries and drugs. In fact, many people heal without any of that. But for me, I began to see a whole spectrum of healing that was directly affecting me in every way for the better.

What I was discovering was miraculous, really. Over time, I created a list of healing options I found and used. Ultimately, I learned that others fighting against the odds were using similar tools to help themselves heal. Eventually, I started to share this information with others in need. I thought that everyone should know. The result is *The Case for Hope*.

This book is dedicated to anyone who might want to learn about the powerful healing connections of the mind, body, and spirit. It's for those fighting illness, their supportive friends and families, and those who are simply looking to live a better life.

My goal was to write a book that was easy to understand and full of facts about the insights and practical methods I had discovered, how they help us, and how to use them. I added examples and stories to keep the information interesting and relatable. I wanted to share these tools so people could know that self-healing is "a thing" and that we can heal many aspects of ourselves with a little guidance in the right direction.

For example, during my healing journey, I learned that extended periods of stress can help create illness. Stress is a big problem for a lot of people. When we use tools to help release or avoid the stress reaction, we give our immune system a great gift toward healing.

I also learned that cancer thrives on sugar and that we can make simple changes in our diet to minimize the problem. I learned relaxation techniques like qigong—an exercise developed in ancient China—and breathing exercises that encourage our blood flow and immune system to thrive and fight illness. I learned that spirituality is not just important, it is vital to living fully.

As *The Case for Hope* begins, in Chapter 1, I share my story, my emotional reaction, my spiritual discovery in the midst of the shock, and the final call-to-arms to fight the illness. This is where the learning began. Ultimately, it is a universal story of healing, as I am not the first and certainly won't be the last in this position.

Chapter 2, "Key Concepts," provides an overview of the potential causes of illness and how healing is generally treated in the United States. Here, we are introduced to the concepts of mind, body, and spirit; the importance of understanding our stress reactions; common challenges with some traditional doctors; and the importance of making positive changes in order to heal.

In chapters 3 and 4, "The Body: 9-1-1" and "More About the Body," I discuss the importance of learning about and reminding ourselves how to improve our wellness using powerful tools like simple breathing techniques, quality sleep, clean water, exercise, the many gifts of healthy foods, and dealing with toxins in our lives.

In chapter 5, "The Mind: Moving Energy to Heal," I point out the many tools that are available to improve health almost immediately by reducing stress and creating a healthier, more balanced nervous system—which, in turn, supports the immune system. These powerful tools include qigong, meditation, guided meditation, prayer, visualization, massage, yoga, acupuncture, music, joy, writing your thoughts, and spending time in nature.

Chapter 6, "The Spirit: Going Deeper," offers an opportunity for deep exploration into the most fundamental aspect of yourself—your soul. Much understanding and growth can happen when we ask for spiritual help from others so we can grow, learn, and heal. As I discuss the need for support from the inside out, I delve into the sticky areas of perspective, judgment, forgiveness, the releasing power of connecting to the soul, and the many gifts that can be found there.

Finally, chapter 7, "Putting It All Together," discusses the aggregate benefit of incorporating all aspects of healing—mind, body, and spirit—to enhance our health, joy, balance, and spiritual awareness. This overview of the concepts in the book is meant to remind you that you can begin creating your own path of healing using the methods discussed in these pages.

It is possible for us to improve our chances to heal, recover, and stay well when we engage with healing tools. This information can be good for anyone.

The message in this book is as simple as it is big: We can heal.

Chapter 1

Waking Up

Awakening is not changing who you are but
discarding who you are not. —Deepak Chopra

It is possible for an event, such as a frightening diagnosis, to awaken us from what we once considered normal, daily activity. It can enable, or perhaps force us to consider our priorities in a different way. We might start with our daily habits, our work life, personal health and our spiritual existence. Alarming events can create an opening to something much deeper in ourselves—a fresh look at our lives. It's a strange reality that for some of us, getting sick might be the only way to wake us up.

What Just Happened?

I am sitting alone in the employee lounge at the MRI facility, waiting for my husband to take me to the hospital. I scan the area. It's replete with extra office supplies—toilet paper, tissues—and a couple of outdated magazines. Clearly, they put me there for my privacy, but also for theirs. In that tortured moment, even I could see that a sobbing woman in the waiting room would probably not be great for business.

I had a moment to think about the news that had been thrust upon me just moments before: "Mrs. Dickenson? I am sorry to tell you this, but your MRI shows that you have a large tumor in your brain. It is cancer, and you need to get someone to take you to the hospital right away. We can't let you drive."

To my credit, I said all of the right things initially. Something like,

"I understand what you are telling me. Are you sure it is cancer? OK. Well, I appreciate that. I needed to know."

I guess I was in shock. But once the message started to filter down to my emotions, I became a bit of a mess, just like millions of others before me who've gotten similar news. My inner monologue went something like this:

Really? This is what I get? Forty-four years old? This is too soon to die! I have two beautiful little girls, my wonderful husband. This cannot be it.

The sorrow set in deep.

At the hospital, doctors confirmed the diagnosis. Brain cancer, grade 3 or 4—the latter being the most aggressive and most likely to spread through the brain quickly. They told me they would have to take a biopsy to be sure which one it was. They explained it was bigger than a golf ball and located above my left ear. It was definitely brain cancer, and fast-growing. I would need to have surgery immediately, and then radiation, and then chemotherapy. Somewhere in the flurry of information, I got the picture that people really die from this—a lot of people. Most people. It was horrific.

Symptoms

I guess it shouldn't have been such a surprise, since I had been experiencing problems for several months. I mostly noticed them while I was working as a lawyer at the law firm I cofounded. I had been practicing law for twenty years, spending most of my time as a transactional lawyer, managing partner, and frequent public speaker on legal issues. (A real snooze, I know.)

Five years earlier, my then-partner and I had decided to leave a well-known firm and take with us a hundred lawyers and staff in a negotiated exit. We were told that we were the largest female-owned real estate law firm, at least in the Southeast. In our new firm, I easily worked seventy hours a week. And I did that for years.

I used to enjoy my work more, especially my clients, but in 2007 and 2008, when the infamous financial breakdown occurred, the challenge and responsibility of managing the firm under those conditions got harder. I began to love it less. In fact, I started to hate it. I had to attend to events that kept me away from what I loved most—the clients and the personal connections. I started to change, and the years of stress began to show. Suffice it to say, I'd been on a tough road for several years before I was diagnosed.

Before I knew I had cancer growing in my brain, I had noticed small things. Like my computer at work seemed painfully bright, so I kept summoning the IT staff to do what they could to reduce the light. I also began to experience extraordinary fatigue and took naps in my car at nearby office parks before I came in to work or after lunch. I was exhausted, even though I was sleeping full nights.

But the worst problem was that I was having trouble finding words, and I was having difficulty reading. I'd have a word on the tip of my tongue, but it wouldn't come. I'd say things like, "What's the name of that restaurant we love so much?" or the mundane "What's that fruit that has spikes on it?" (starfruit). I was doing this all the time—but not just for mundane things. I'd forget some of my big clients' names. Or even toward the end, I could not recall the names of some of the lawyers and employees in the firm.

I'd force my staff and family into a spontaneous game of modified charades. I could describe the people or things but was not able to name them. I'd get annoyed by my victims' lack of quick responses as they tirelessly tried to figure out what in the world I was looking for. Obviously, as I would learn later, the part of my brain that controls memory was being pressured by the cancerous tumor, limiting my ability to recall basic names and words. All the while, the tumor continued to grow at a fast pace.

In addition to the memory issues, I began to have problems reading quickly. In fact, if I didn't have a lot of time to read something, I would grab one of the other lawyers to read it for me. Now, my ability to receive the information they read to me was pristine. I knew exactly how to handle the problem or issue. I was quick to remember previous situations and their details. I was also able to communicate the information in a very cogent and lucid way and explain what it meant and what we needed to do about it. That was not a problem. The problem was that I just couldn't read it very well for myself.

I went to a neurologist, a doctor that studies the brain, and told him about my symptoms. After a cursory assessment, his pronouncement was, "Most lawyers are stressed right now." He suggested that stress might be the cause of my word-finding issues and slow reading. He wasn't too concerned. Almost as an afterthought, he ordered an EEG, a test where electrodes are attached to the head to measure brain-wave activity. It would be administered at home for three days.

Much later, I came to understand that it was, among other things, primarily a test for seizures. Apparently, the doctor suspected that might be what was going on with me, although he did not say as much at that time. Regardless, the company that was supposed to administer the test was not immediately available because they were moving. They told me they would get back with me when they could. It was mid-March when we talked, and I warned them I would be traveling for business in May. Of course they were ready to perform the test just as I was ready to go on my business trips, which forced me to delay the test further.

Because of the neurologist's nonchalant reaction to my symptoms, I figured the problem was my eyesight. Maybe it was time for me to get those cheaters that everyone seems to need the day they turn forty. So I went to the eye doctor and tried to press him on my other issues, but he assured me that it was because I was no spring chicken at the age of forty-four. All I needed to do was get reading glasses so I could see properly. As I left his office, I called my husband and tearfully told him the great news that I only needed cheaters to solve my problem. On a deeper level, however, both of us felt it wasn't over.

Armed with my new readers, I presented a speech at the annual seminar for fellow lawyers. The night before my presentation, as I was preparing my notes, I had the strange feeling that I was losing the information. I *knew* the information, but the more I would make notes in the margins, the more it felt like it was vanishing from my memory. So I would make more notes in the margins. It was as if the information was new, and I couldn't hold on to it.

The next day, I was concerned, but with a standing-room-only crowd, I was hoping for the best. The first minute was pure agony as I shuffled with my written notes, struggling to make sense of them. I made a joke about my new cheaters and put my useless notes down. I performed the entire hour perfectly from memory.

Two weeks later, I had another speech to give for another annual professional group meeting. But this time, I was not so lucky. I couldn't perform even close to what I would have liked. Worse, it was obvious to my audience. Once I got home from the seminar (it was a six-hour drive), I demanded an MRI from my neurologist. I had to fight for it, too—my doctor was insisting that we try other procedures first.

I learned later that some doctors won't immediately arrange for MRIs because the tests are expensive, and the doctors don't usually make any money on them. Whether that was the case or not, I will never know. However, the tumor was growing quickly by then. I sometimes wonder how much damage would have been avoided if he had recommended an MRI from the outset. Regardless, my insistence finally bore fruit as he relented and ordered the MRI. So there I was at the MRI place waiting for my husband to take me to the hospital while fearing the worst.

Moment of Clarity

It turns out the greatest things in life aren't things at all.

On my first day in the hospital, I had a moment of clarity—and something was forever changed in me. I was crying with my next-door neighbor and friend, who also happened to be a nurse and had worked with brain-cancer patients. Coincidentally, her husband was a brain surgeon. He, too, was at the hospital, talking to the doctors to help us out. Turns out, my next-door neighbors were extremely knowledgeable about brain cancer. You just can't make this stuff up!

My friend wasn't sugarcoating the situation for me. "This is bad," she said. "This is really, really bad." In her arms, hearing the truth, I said a prayer for the first time in a long time. Not sure I was doing it right, I prayed to God with all my heart to let me live. I promised to honor the covenants (yes, I really used that word) I had made to my husband and children to prioritize them and myself, and to change my life to focus on the things that really matter. It was so clear. That was my path, my earnest promise, and I would honor it.

With that, everything in my life outside of my family melted away in importance: my firm, my work, my accomplishments. I had no pride associated with those things. This clarity allowed me to see how I had been mismanaging my life. I had been out of whack. I had not known how to fix it, so I just kept moving forward the way I always did. I had spent so much time focusing on my work even though, ultimately, it meant nothing to me. I had the profound sense that I already had everything I needed and wanted.

Although true, my new awareness was strange, and I was surprised by it. It seemed to foster an immediate restructuring of my life. By calling out for help in prayer and seeking my truth, I received a deep sense that there was something bigger for me. There was a path I could follow.

Later that night, a battering rainstorm pounded my hospital windows like a freakish car wash, strangely mirroring my emotions. I wondered, as they do symbolically in the movies, if the storm was an omen, representing bad things ahead, or maybe it was a cleansing, offering an opportunity to try this life thing again in a different way. I had no idea which one it was.

The Learning Begins

The next day, the doctors took a biopsy of my brain to get more information about the depth and quality of the cancer. They did not remove the rest of the cancerous tumor, however.

For some reason, it took them eight grueling days to send me the results. The delay was torturous, because I knew the tumor was growing quickly and that it was important to get it removed as soon as possible to avoid additional damage. The only thing positive about it was that it gave my husband and me the time to process what it all meant. During that time, I began to learn some of the tools that I share later in this book that helped me get through the ordeal.

I was unwilling to search the internet for information about my new diagnosis. I was terrified to read about what I really had and my chances with it. Also, at that point, the tumor was causing so much pressure on my brain that it was hard to read and comprehend anything easily. Thankfully, my brother and my mom weren't as squeamish about doing the online research, and they dove in and gave me a lot of information —sanitized for my benefit, I'm sure.

My mom learned that cancer thrives on sugar, so I immediately cut out all processed sugar. My brother sent me a DVD of a form of Chinese meditation for healing called qigong (sounds like "chee-gong") and breathing techniques he found on the internet. When I got it, I could not have understood how critical these things would be for me. I used them faithfully every day, and they gave me a sense of peace from the anticipated brain surgery, radiation, chemotherapy, and general drive to figure out how to manage it all. I discovered an incredible sense of peace from qigong and the breathing techniques.

My brother also sent me a guided meditation CD that helped me visualize a wellness that belied my present circumstances. That was very powerful for me too. If I hadn't had those basic tools to lean on, I would have only had the shock, sadness, and extreme fear of my predicament. I truly believe that getting those tools *early in the process* provided a powerful way for me to start healing even before the surgery and treatments could begin. Taking control of one's illness is a powerful way to start healing.

We finally got the call about the biopsy results, and the doctor said that the tumor was a glioblastoma multiform, grade 4, meaning the worst form of it, although none of it is good. He said I needed surgery immediately. Even though the updated news was terrible, the waiting period—and some of the tools I had learned to use—helped me to understand that there was something beyond the illness for me. Hope was very much with me. Despite the doctor's prognosis, I began to change my view of what was possible for me.

The brain surgery was successful. The doctor wouldn't confirm that he got all of the cancer, but it appeared to me from the MRI that he had. My doctor warned me that my type of cancer often comes back quickly, so he recommended that I take the radiation and chemo as planned. So I did.

Although the surgery seemed to have been very successful, the doctors didn't give me the impression that I had won the lottery. In fact, I would learn later that this kind of cancer typically comes back in a short period of time with a vengeance, offering a dismal life expectancy rate of twelve to eighteen months. For those who beat those survival rates, less than 5 percent will survive more than five years. Understandably, the doctors did not seem to have a lot of hope for me. They told me to try not to think about it. I should just enjoy life. But how do you live with a diagnosis like that?

I decided to ignore what they were implying and committed myself to becoming one of the people who survives anyway. I believed I had a fighting chance to beat the cancer. *Why not me?* I thought. Refusing to define myself by my illness was powerful and an important decision for my journey of self-healing. There were many times that the doctors told me the cancer would come back, and I won't lie, those words would get stuck in my head. But I'd eventually shake it off, thinking, *They don't know what is possible for me. All they know are statistics. Don't look to them for hope—they don't have any.*

I began fighting for what I believed—not the odds. Here's the thing: how many people don't fight? Many people don't know about the self-healing ammo available to fight cancer, to fight other illnesses, and to find happiness. How many out there make the words of their doctors and the statisticians their only source of hope? If I had believed the stats and the doctors, I would not have journeyed to find the rich healing modalities that I now believe helped heal me. Without the power and willingness to consider different outcomes, it's likely I would not be here to tell this story.

Fortunately, the surgery lessened the pressure in the memory and language centers of my brain. Once the swelling went down some, I worked with a speech and language pathologist for a year and a half to get as much of my reading and memory skills back as possible. The effort made an enormous difference in my ability to read and learn more about healing myself.

Because I was very open to what I was learning about, my healing process became very organic. Even more importantly, I began to understand that, whether or not I beat my illness, I was choosing to live a life worth living anyway.

Why This Book

Hope is not a guarantee ... but it's an awfully good place to start.

When I started getting stronger both physically and psychologically, I worked in earnest to learn more about certain healing tools. I knew how much qigong, the breathing techniques, and the physical exercises were helping me, and I had a healthy understanding of how the food I chose to eat was enabling me to fight the cancer.

Once I started to go deeper in my research about healing, I started to understand and feel the intimate connection of mind, body, and spirit. In addition to the coincidences I experienced on this journey (which could fill their own book), I began to believe my path was genuinely inspired. I would stumble into one healing area just as I needed it, and then another and another, right on cue. It was as if I was in a personal master class created to help me live beyond the diagnosis and get me to the place meant for me. I was open to what was coming in, and I believed in hope.

I can now better understand the wisdom in my stumbling around. But as I was searching for and discovering tools to help me heal, I started getting frustrated that I couldn't seem to find any comprehensive books that encapsulated the basic healing techniques I was learning about. It wasn't until much later that I would discover a few self-healing books that incorporated mind, body, and spirit together, but I didn't find them until I had figured it out first on my own—at which point, they served as a beautiful and reassuring confirmation of the journey I had been following.

I was finding books about yoga that seemed to promise the means to healing. Then I noticed that the books about exercise and healthy food seemed to do the same. Yet again, there were meditation books that suggested they had the answers to life's healing questions. I began to recognize that the truth was multifaceted, like a diamond; it couldn't be confined within the limitations of the individual books I was reading. I was beginning to understand that healing involves many parts of ourselves; and the body, the spirit, and the mind all need time to heal completely.

Through this process, I was reminded that we are meant to heal ourselves. We do it all the time, after all. Like when we get a cold or a bruise, or even when we say "I'm sorry" and mean it.

As I received the benefits of the tools I was using, my awareness grew, and I started to feel compelled to share what I was learning. All of the things I was doing were so simple yet so powerful—especially when done in combination with each other. My new techniques and habits were changing my biorhythms and enabling me to heal.

I felt an enormous sense of gratitude that, for whatever reason, a healing path had opened up before me and I was able to receive it and absorb it. I felt deeply that it was helping to heal the many parts of myself.

But it did make me mad that every single person doesn't know about all of this! So I had a new goal of getting the basic information that I was learning out to as many people as possible. I was beating the odds, and I wanted other people to know how they could do it too. I wanted to reach the people who don't know that self-healing is real. I wanted to share my story so that it might become a springboard to a greater story—a universal story about healing.

This is the book I wish I'd had when I was diagnosed—or even before that. This is the purpose of *The Case for Hope*.

Chapter 2

Key Concepts: How We Can Heal

Anything that increases the efficiency of the healing system or helps it neutralize harmful influences will increase the probability of spontaneous healing.
—Andrew Weil, MD, Spontaneous Healing

I believe that illness might be a result of reactions from systems in the body, mind, and/or spirit that have been out of balance for a long period of time. I consider those three parts—the mind (what we think about), body (the physical body), and spirit (the belief in something bigger than ourselves)—to be the three pillars of our health. When any of them are out of balance, disease can manifest in the body as a result.

If when mind, body, and spirit are not in balance, illness can result, why can't the opposite be true? Why can't restoring balance to these systems heal us and make us well again? Not only do I believe that it can, I am proof of it. I have also personally met, listened to, and read countless stories of other survivors who have healed from life-threatening illnesses and live healthy lives, defying the odds. They have come to the same conclusion that I have: that the sum of the parts—the three pillars—can create balance and put us back on a healing road to wellness.

When we learn to focus on these three essential aspects of ourselves, we can be empowered toward physical healing, emotional support, and spiritual wisdom. And when we begin to harness these aspects of ourselves, anything is possible.

The World We Live In

Our eyes are open, but we can't see.

We live in a world that can easily overwhelm us with things that we don't really need, and too little of what we desperately do need: space, peace, and a sense of harmony. Our lives have been forever changed as a result of the modern technological society we live in. Some of the change is good; a lot is bad.

Our mind, body, and spirit were not meant for the volume of information and the rate of change most of us experience these days—and most people are unable to handle it all. We are witnessing an epidemic of drug abuse even in children, as they take the drugs just to get through the day. Yet we feed them a constant diet of sugar-filled processed food and give them unlimited access to technology while offering little incentive for them to run and play outside.

In the United States, studies indicate that more than 50 percent of divorces are caused or hastened by one partner's obsessive interest in pornographic websites.[1] Easy access to porn sites can give men and women (and now, young teenagers as well) impossible standards of physical intimacy to fulfill and can impede their ability for real connection with people they love. Don't think for a minute that this isn't big business—it is. But at what cost?

More and more, people who go out to eat at restaurants spend a great deal of their time on their phones instead of talking with their dining partners—who are doing the same thing. They could be sharing their day and observing what is around them together. But they live in a partially engaged life, at best. It's as if this is an addiction—and it just might be.

Devices can be vices that keep people away from personal connection. Paradoxically, their ubiquitous presence feeds a cycle of loneliness in a world of people hungry for real connection. To compound the problem, our culture has sucked most of us into a full-blown environment of consumerism, and many accept it as normal. The outlets of technology (TV, internet, phones, tablets, etc.) are constantly marketing to us with the promise that our lives will be so much better if we purchase this or that product or service.

The underlying message to the consumer is: you have a hole, and this or that product will fill it. We're told the product or service will satisfy us—make us happy and somehow fulfilled. Many are taken in by it. But these are false promises and are always broken. Simply put, *things* can't make us truly happy, they can only make us *feel* happy temporarily. These are two very different realities. The truth is, spending money may fill some things but never the soul.

If we don't have something to help us counter the constant messages, we become lost, like leaves floating in the air. Many people feel sad and empty, not knowing why. But there is hope. We must go deep within ourselves to find our happiness, tranquility, and balance and to counteract the insanity around us. It's there that we can discover the truth we have had all along. It is ready for us if we are willing to learn how to find it.

There are two antidotes to offset the manipulation, frenzy, and noise of the commercialized, technology-driven world we live in. The first is to simply turn it all off—the smartphones, the internet, the computers, all of it, at least for a while. Step away and sit in silence, go outside, walk around in nature, and breathe deeply. Unplug and relax. Even though it might feel strange at first, I know that you will begin to feel better, even relieved. I like to say, "Use technology, but don't let it use you." Unplugging is a way we can remind ourselves how to stop it from using us.

The second antidote is to learn about and integrate new tools, such as the ones I describe in this book. These tools—including clean eating, good sleep habits, meditation, breathing techniques, the joy of music, yoga, and qigong—will show you how to be balanced, peaceful, and feel a sense of wholeness. It can also be very powerful to explore the higher aspects of yourself by reaching out to God, the universe. Even the simple act of prayer can help you discover deep truths and healing. When we are anchored with gifts of mind, body, and spirit, we are no longer like a leaf floating in the wind, uncertain and reactive. We are more like a tree—grounded and strong.

Managing Stress

Stress is a significant problem for many people. In our harried lives, it has become difficult to avoid. But not all stress is bad. A helpful stress reaction protects us against real danger, like confronting a bear in the woods. It's just that we are not built to withstand constant stress. Over time, it can cause damage to our health.

At its core, the fight-or-flight reaction is the expression of a primitive part of the brain that doesn't have any in-betweens: it's either on or off. When it's on, the body and brain jump into hyperdrive to save us from potential death. When it's off, we are balanced and calm.

The problem is that in our present society, many of us experience high levels of stress with little awareness of the primal purpose of the stress reaction—to fight against a mortal threat. We get stressed about being late, traffic, money, kids, family, work ... I don't really have to list them all. You already know where the stress comes from!

Sometimes we call them *frustrations, anxiety, worry,* or *alarm.* Whatever word you use, the body reacts in the same way. When we treat daily situations as if they warrant the full fight-or-flight reaction, we tax our system unnecessarily. Ultimately, living this way can take a great toll on the body and result in disease.

"Dis-ease" is a lack of ease that affects the body, the mind, and often the spirit, putting the body out of balance. Chronic stress has been shown to be harmful to the muscles, respiratory system, cardiovascular system, endocrine system, adrenal glands, liver, gastric system, and nervous system. It is linked to six of the leading causes of death: heart disease, cancer, lung ailments, accidents, cirrhosis of the liver, and suicide.[2] Weakened by constant stress, the body has a harder time fending off diseases. So, instead of your immune system being strong and effective against illness, infection, abnormalities, toxins, and cancer cells, it gets derailed and overwhelmed, allowing miscreants like cancer cells to gain a foothold and find a hospitable home in which to thrive.

The body's autonomic nervous system is what regulates most of our bodily functions. It is made up of two parts that have very different roles to play. The sympathetic nervous system is like the emergency system that responds when we are in danger or when we get really angry. It starts pumping the hormone cortisol, which is the body's wake-up call that we need to fight or flee because danger is upon us. The pupils of the eyes and the bronchi in the lungs dilate, the heart rate accelerates, the ability to salivate is inhibited, and the digestive system contracts in preparation for the imminent threat.

The parasympathetic nervous system, on the other hand—sometimes called "rest and digest"—slows down the body's functions and conserves energy. When a stress event is over, the parasympathetic system steps in and helps the body resume normal functions. This system is in play when we are calm and relaxed, and our body systems work normally without stresses from actual or perceived danger. Not surprisingly, many of us in our Western culture have nervous systems stuck in "on" mode, braced for fight-or-flight from all the stress, with the sympathetic nervous system in control.

As I have unofficially identified the cause of my illness—consistent stress for a period of almost five years—this topic is of particular interest to me. I had no idea that I was running down my body and my mind. But once I got sick, I discovered many ways to lessen my stress reactions in order to support health.

Stress can be compared to wearing a heavy backpack. The weight can be overbearing. Now imagine removing some of the heaviness to reduce your stress. Breathe deep and let go. I believe we're not meant to live jam-packed lives or to live surrounded by toxic people and events. I believe we are meant to live in balance as much as possible. The process begins with becoming more aware of the causes of stress in our lives and taking a hard look at how we can reduce it for our own health and wellness.

Some Thoughts About Traditional Western Medicine

I have to admit that I have conflicting feelings about traditional Western medicine. While I have benefited greatly from it, I have also witnessed its limitations.

For all of the time, money, education, and training our traditional Western doctors invest in their work, most of them (*but not all*) still have blind spots that inhibit their ability to heal their patients optimally and thoroughly. Their blind spots often include having little interest in the root cause of disease, permanent healing, keeping an open mind when it comes to healing, and spending time with their patients and listening to them. Most fall short when it comes to understanding nutrition and recognizing that their patients' thoughts and life experiences can play an important role in helping them heal properly.

Too often, doctors rush in and out of appointments, give patients medicine, and offer surgeries instead of trying less-invasive solutions first. And in their flurry, many of them have no idea about the true cause of the illness—and apparently, no interest in it either. But when doctors are curious about why a person may have gotten sick, there is an opportunity to improve the interaction between doctor and patient, allowing for potential clues that might lead to healing.

Considering the epidemic of cancer in the United States, for example, I'd say it's time to take a good look at causation. But generally, that's not what seems to be happening in traditional Western medicine. Instead, this camp seems to be resistant to change and unwilling to even learn from the success brought forth by alternative forms of medicine and healing. Even osteopaths and integrative medicine doctors—fully licensed medical doctors focused on a whole-body approach to healing—are sometimes looked down upon by Western physicians.

To be fair, part of it may be because traditional Western doctors are fearful that alternative healing will harm their patients. On the other hand, their fear might be due to the fact that most traditional Western MDs don't know very much about alternatives, including the power of good nutrition. That might make it easier for them to dismiss alternative healing outright—because they don't know about it.

Another possibility is that some involved in traditional Western medicine might fear that alternative healing practices, which are becoming big business, could threaten them economically. If people discover they can sometimes heal themselves without drugs and surgery, it's not hard to see how the MDs might be negatively affected.

In her book *An American Sickness*, Elizabeth Rosenthal describes in great detail the grim reality of traditional Western medicine, the pharmaceutical companies, the American Medical Association (AMA), and the US government. From a profit perspective, she concludes, there appears to be little motivation for doctors and pharmaceutical companies to cure their patients outright.[3]

Rosenthal explains that the medical system is set up for physicians to provide surgeries and medicines to help us get *well enough* to keep taking the medicines and keep coming to the doctor's office instead of solving the root cause of the problem and becoming healed.[4] In this way, it is not hard to argue that some of us are becoming the victims of a business-first-healing-second approach, as Rosenthal notes.

Obviously, the system is not working very well for many of us. Therefore, it is critical that we keep our eyes open and take control of our healing path. Theoretically, there is no one more invested in our health than us. We must be our own best advocates.

In *The Healing Power of Sound*,[5] author Mitchell Gaynor, an MD and oncologist with top medical credentials, describes his frustration when his cancer patients were not doing as well as he wanted. When one patient came in looking particularly better than normal, he quizzed the man about the change. The patient had been going to a "healer"—a non-MD offering alternative healing options—and felt he was getting better as a result. In fact, the growth of his disease had stopped abruptly.

Dr. Gaynor was curious, and he researched some of the methods his patient was using. He concluded that if something works for one patient, then maybe it could help the others, too. His goal was nothing less than to *cure* his patients.

What he discovered opened him up to other forms of healing, which allowed him to offer the best possible care and optimal results for his patients. By using some of these methods along with his traditional medical practice, he helped his patients significantly improve. Dr.

Gaynor writes, "I have long since come to accept nontraditional, holistic approaches as necessities, rather than potential options, that must be integrated with the care and treatment of my patients."[6]

Dr. Andrew Weil shares a similar understanding about healing in his New York Times best seller *Spontaneous Healing*. Weil, a graduate of Harvard Medical School and one of the most influential practitioners of holistic care, states that Western doctors "tend to disbelieve the stories [about healing] without attempting to verify them."[7] He writes, "People can get better. More than that, they can get better from all sorts of conditions of disease, even very severe ones of long duration."[8] He continues, "The evidence is incontrovertible that the body is capable of healing itself. By ignoring that, many doctors cut themselves off from a tremendous source of optimism about health and healing."[9]

If physicians and medical institutions are unwilling to embrace the efficacy of the healing tools available to us, I believe they are still obligated to at least direct their patients toward additional healing choices. But, for whatever reason, some doctors don't say anything about it. And the silence is deafening.

Patients who unquestioningly trust everything a doctor says would conclude that this silence must mean there is nothing else to know about their care. In this way, the omission is the offense. The patient leaves the office with incomplete information coming from a confident MD who appears to have all the answers. Care is à la carte. It's just that the patient doesn't know it.

Even worse than the silence might be when doctors flat-out give bad information. Cancer specialists have told me that incorporating the spice turmeric in our food or in liquid or capsule supplements is a waste of time from a health perspective. But the truth is, a significant amount of research has linked turmeric (*curcuma longa*) and curcumin (the active component often associated with its yellow pigment) with anti-inflammatory properties, not to mention antioxidant and even anti-cancer properties as well.[10,11,12] It's noteworthy that many turmeric supplements contain *piperine*, a compound in black pepper, which enhances the absorption of curcumin.[13]

Keeping inflammation low can be critical in fighting cancer and many other types of illnesses. Inflammation in the body forces the cells to fight the cause of the inflammation. While the fighting cells are busy managing inflammation, they can't completely focus on other threats, such as those sneaky cancer cells. That's why turmeric can be a great friend anytime, but especially when we are fighting cancer. Reducing inflammation is critical when it comes to healing.

I once asked one of my doctors what suggestions he had for me about using good nutrition to help fight the cancer. He told me that since I looked like I was in good shape, I should just keep doing whatever I was doing. Ugh.

It's bad when they silently suggest they have all the answers but don't, and it's also bad when they give us bad information that we might rely on. But the one thing that some MDs do that really gets me the most is when they take hope from a person. I know the odds may not be in a patient's favor, but there is always hope, as small as it may be, and I strongly object to anyone taking that away from someone.

I was referred to a man several years ago who had been diagnosed with grade 4 brain cancer, just like mine. He was unable to have surgery due to the location of the cancer in his brain, but he did get chemotherapy and radiation. When I met with him to share what I had learned in my fight, he felt like he had little hope, even with the chemo and radiation planned. The doctors had told him the same thing my doctors had told me: "Get your affairs in order. This will not end well."

I spent time on the phone with him and then met with him and his wife in person, pouring out as much information as I could about my own path of healing. That night, he and his wife emailed to say how thankful they were for our time together and the fact that, for the first time, someone had given them a glimmer of hope. It meant a lot to both of them.

After that, he dove into the tools we had discussed. Eight months later, his tests showed a 50 percent reduction of the cancer—a rate that his doctors had never seen before. Today, four years from his diagnosis, he is still going strong with stable results.

I feel strongly that no one has the right to take anyone's hope away—yet I know that it happens every day. I believe, especially when we get very sick, it's for us to find hope, knowing our traditional doctor may not be willing or able to supply it. Some of the doctors may not believe in it or might just see you as a statistic. Either way, it is often important for healing to stretch beyond what doctors tell you and start believing in yourself.

With a little bit of hope, you might start to think, *You know, if some people can survive the shitstorm I'm in, why can't I?* Just that kernel of a thought can begin to change things. It's a glimmer of hope. And then you can take the first step. You open a book about healing and living instead of obsessing over life-expectancy statistics. Maybe it is bad. Maybe you don't have to obsess about that. Maybe you have different plans for yourself.

How to Work with Doctors

Before you go to your next doctor's appointment, you might want to do some of the following things to make sure you get what you need from the visit:

1. **Bring a list of questions.** I recommend preparing a list a couple of days before your doctor's appointment, since questions often seem to come and go during a normal day.
2. **Make sure the doctor answers your questions to your satisfaction, and write down the explanation right then and there.** Too often, we don't understand the explanation a doctor gives us, and then we think we're the problem or we're not smart enough to understand it. So we don't pursue an explanation, and we pretend we did understand. Be respectful but do keep asking until you understand what the doctor is trying to say. Try, "I didn't understand that. Please explain that again." Doctors often default to speaking at a level that only another doctor can understand. But that's not fair to you.

You can't be expected to know what doctors know. That's why you go to them for advice. It's their job to explain, in simple language, what you don't understand.

3. **Stand up for yourself and be your own advocate.** Doctors can play an important part in your healing process, but they haven't cornered the market on healing. Sometimes we just know what is right for us and we should feel comfortable sharing the information with our doctor, our partner in healing.

   When I was six months into chemotherapy, I had a strong sense that any benefit the chemotherapy offered had been achieved, but now it was just wearing down my body and system. The doctors wanted me to take it for twelve months and wouldn't agree to letting me stop taking the chemo. Amazingly, in the ninth month, I developed a strong allergic reaction to the medicine. In response, my doctor wanted to pump me up with steroids so I could keep taking the chemo, but fortunately, I dug deeper.

   I learned that the manufacturer of the product only suggests a course of six months, based on its trials. Apparently, the twelve-month concept became a practice of oncologists just to ostensibly ensure the chemo would blast the cancer. The thing is, the chemo blasts everything—the very bad and the very good. With this information, I was able to convince my doctors that it was time to stop the chemo, and they agreed. Finally, I was able to start healing my body from the ravages of the chemotherapy and everything else I had been through.

4. **Be your own scientist.** Sometimes when you tell doctors about a problem, they'll tell you nothing is wrong, or my favorite, "There is nothing you can do." While we don't want to be paranoid, sometimes those perfunctory responses are not appropriate. If you don't get to the bottom of the problem, it can sometimes manifest into something bigger. Observing your body, researching independently, noticing correlations between the symptoms and other things occurring, and

getting another opinion are all wise things to do for your health. For example, if your eye begins to twitch, you might think about when the twitching happens. Are you tired? Are you stressed? Asking your own questions and eliminating others can go a long way to solving the mystery.

5. **Remember that your medical records are *your* medical records.** It is a good practice to get copies of your complete medical records as you proceed, including those for MRIs, CT scans, and doctors' notes and analyses. When your blood is tested, be sure you get a copy of the results. This information keeps you in control. If you want to get another opinion, change your doctor, or review some of the notes or test results, you have the information you need. Under HIPAA, the Health Insurance Portability and Accountability Act of 1996, patients have a right to receive their medical records no later than thirty days from the request, and the information is to be provided in the format requested by the patient (for example, paper copy, fax, electronic copy, or CD), if possible. You might have to pay a small charge, but it is worth it if you are able. Remember: knowledge is power. No one is more invested in your health than you.

The Healing Power of Change

It's called a wake-up call for a reason.

Everyone is unique. But if you get sick and do nothing to improve your environment or your mindset, why should you expect improved results? Getting sick provides us with an opportunity to weed out negative, stressful areas of our lives as much as possible and create an environment that supports a healthy mind, body, and spirit. It's an opportunity to rebuild ourselves with a stronger structure than we had ever thought possible.

Repurposing the challenges in our lives into wisdom, love, and peace is a goal that is within our grasp. Doing so can offer great gifts that can change us for the better.

I'm convinced that people who get sick and make systemic mind, body, spirit, and life changes are more effective at fighting illness and maintaining their health afterward than those who do not. Life changes can include improving your diet, exercising, and using the other tools I share in this book. They can also include removing negative people from your environment or your work situation. Even letting people help you can be a life change if you are the kind of person who takes care of others but has a hard time accepting care for yourself.

Right after suffering from a serious illness—and even during it—some people rush right back to what they were doing before their diagnosis. They don't consider how they got sick in the first place. If they don't focus on continued health and awareness, sometimes they get more sick, symptoms return, or they even develop a new illness. It takes time to get really sick. It makes sense that we give ourselves plenty of time to heal, too.

Several years ago, I put my peace lily plant (*spathiphyllum*) in a pot outside, watered it, and took care of it. For a long time, it looked like it was doing well, but then the leaves began to be stressed with burn marks. I tried to add more water and then less water. Nothing seemed to work. It didn't look healthy anymore, and I started to think it might be time to end its suffering and give it to the big dumpster in the sky. Peace Lily was doomed.

But I decided to give it one more chance. I made some changes. I cut down all of the dead leaves. I was careful with the consistency of the water (not too much, not too little). I brought the plant back inside and put it near a window that had some sunlight, but not too much.

The plant became invigorated by its new environment and care. After a few weeks, it had transformed. The leaves were beautiful and a deep green—not stressed, brown, and wilting like they had been before. The whole plant perked up; it was like new. A plant miracle! Once I figured out what made it happy, I was careful to take good care of it just as I had when I was bringing it back to life. As a result, Peace Lily lives on.

This simple story illustrates the importance of making permanent, healthy changes in our lives, especially when we get seriously sick. But it can also apply to those of us experiencing a deep sense that something is just not right in our lives, such as excessive stress, frustration, anger, and repressed emotions. We are not built to feel these kinds of feelings all the time. If you are grappling with life stressors, you have a unique chance to make healthy changes *before* illness steps in.

When it comes to illness, however, it is important to manage your reactions and plan how you are going to move forward. In these cases, there is a timing element that doesn't apply to healthy people looking to improve their lives generally. Illness is often urgent. As a result, when you're ill, it can be a good time to take a hard look at how you are choosing to live your life, with a healthy dose of truth and honesty. Think about the good things you like the most in your life that are not unhealthy and do more of that. Then think about the things in your life that are hurtful, painful, or constantly negative and remove them from your life or find a way to manage them in a healthy way so they won't hurt you any further.

At one of my talks, I met a man who had been diagnosed with grade 4 glioblastoma, as I had been, and he was working a full-time, stressful job. He didn't love his job, and he didn't have to work if he didn't want to. He was developing additional health issues in other parts of his brain in addition to his cancerous tumor.

I asked him if he had considered stopping work and really focusing on healing only. He said "Yes, but I would just be bored. I like to keep busy."

I looked at his wife. She was frustrated because she had been pleading with him to stop working and focus on healing. I didn't say what I wanted to say, and maybe I should have. But what I wanted to say was that you only have one shot at throwing everything you have at fighting this illness. Why in the world would you spend what just might be your last months of life working if you didn't love it and you didn't need to do it for financial reasons? This is it. And even if you have to work during your illness, you can still implement changes in your life to increase your chances of beating it.

For some people, work is not the problem. Sometimes they have issues with their life or their spouse or family members. These are negative influences in their life. Self-healing in these situations might require limiting access to people like that.

One woman I knew was diagnosed with breast cancer and, although she and her husband didn't have the best marriage, she was hoping he would rise to the occasion and be supportive. She told me he was helpful, but he didn't exactly provide the kind of support she needed. The experience helped her recognize the deep-rooted problems they had together and how the relationship was negatively affecting her. Seeing that caused her to change her perspective about the marriage. Later, when she was ready, she divorced him. Although the process was difficult, she knew that letting go of the toxic relationship was part of her healing path.

Of course, not everyone who fights serious illnesses (children, for example) will necessarily have a cause and effect that they can point to. But many people do find things beyond the diagnoses that have been bringing them down for a long time. Maybe you might realize, like my peace lily, that it's time to make some changes so you can flourish again.

Engage Your Will

> *The journey of a thousand miles begins with a single step.*—*Chinese philosopher Lao Tzu (circa 531 BCE)*

I don't believe there is a way to discover the path of healing without engaging your will to be well. In life, our will and loving determination can make all the difference. When we choose to invoke the will, we choose not once, or twice, but all the time, every day, every moment. Ultimately, it becomes completely natural, incorporated into your life and who you are as if it has always been there. In this way, you transform from the caterpillar to the butterfly.

So keep your mind open as you discover the many different tools in this book and others you might find that support your path to health. You are very important, and you are entitled to become the very best version of yourself. *It is possible.* Believe in yourself and believe that you have the power to change. There is no magic pill, and nobody else can do it but you. Every moment is an opportunity to engage your will to create the changes you wish for. Amazing things can happen. This book can show you how.

Our bodies are our gardens to which our
wills are gardeners.—Shakespeare

Chapter 3

The Body: 9-1-1

When we get sick or discover a potential health problem, it can feel like a 9-1-1 emergency—and it might just be. When these kinds of events happen to most of us, taking care of our body suddenly gets placed front and center. The doctor might say that you need to exercise, lose weight, or eat right. But if you haven't been doing that already, the instructions from the doctor might just put you into a tailspin as you wonder how you're going to figure all of that out. You might ask yourself, *Is this really the time to restructure everything I've been doing in my life and, at the same time, deal with a potentially life-threatening illness?*

The answer is, well, yes!

Although it can be overwhelming to realize we need a crash course in supporting our bodies and turning the ship in a better direction, there is a way to do just that. And it is not just for people who find themselves a little behind the eight ball. These tools are for all those who want to make fundamental changes in their bodies— and, hopefully, their mind and spirit too, since it's all connected (as you will learn later in this book).

As you develop the tools to build a healthier body in this section and the next, you will see how you can begin to improve your health almost immediately. This is because these practices are basic and fundamental to health and healthy living.

When you find ways to use these tools and maximize their benefits, you might be surprised and excited by what you discover is possible for you, your body, your self-confidence, and your health. Whether you are in a 9-1-1 situation that you need to attend to urgently or you realize you just need to make some changes in your life for the better, this section and the next offer some easy ways to remind yourself how to do just that.

How to Breathe

Breathing and breath are described as *breath and spirit, life source,* and *vital energy* in many cultures around the world. These descriptions point to a deep understanding and respect for breath—as they should. Our first breath happens when we are born, and our last happens upon our death. We can't live without breathing. Yet we rarely think about it because it happens automatically. When we incorporate conscious breathing, breathing techniques, or *qi* breathing, we give ourselves the opportunity to expand the breath. The results can be powerful.

Breathing techniques have been in existence for thousands of years as a way for people to tap into their life energy. Breathing with conscious intention can be a simple yet impactful way to be present with ourselves, feel calm and relaxed, process emotions, recharge, listen to our intuition, and sharpen our mind. Using breath in this way can allow us a respite to feel safe and joyful, adding optimism to our lives and environment. It also supports the immune system and helps to balance the three pillars of health—body, mind and spirit.

When we breathe, we take in oxygen (O_2), which energizes our cells, tissues and organs and helps improve blood flow. We breathe out carbon dioxide (CO_2), which removes toxins and waste from our bodies. Exercise, vigorous activity, yoga, meditation, qigong, and breathing techniques can make the most of the breathing process.

Breathing exercises can also impact cancer because cancer cells can't thrive in a highly oxygenated environment. Exercise and breathing techniques can help create an oxygenated environment, which supports the immune system that fights against cancer cells and other abnormal cells.

However, it's important to note that a cancer cell can switch to an anaerobic system that makes it possible for the cancer cell to no longer rely on oxygen to live.[14] Instead of oxygen, the cancer cell relies on glucose (sugar) for its energy. In this way, the effect of exercise and breathing practices won't have as much, or any, effect on a cancer cell that has made this change. Still, intentional breathing practices remain an important tool we can use to help our immune system gobble up troublemakers we don't want in our body and enhance other aspects of ourselves, so we are healthier and happier.

I started to use breathing techniques soon after I was diagnosed, and they quickly became some of the most important healing tools I would discover. I used them every morning and night to calm me, support my body, and create space in my mind. When I am stressed or particularly worried, I use these methods because they calm my nervous system. Breathing techniques work, they are free, and they can be done almost anywhere.

There are many ways to breathe, and some are better than others. Shallow breathing, for example, usually happens when we feel stressed or panicked. But people who don't exercise or practice breathing techniques and those who engage only their chest and not their solar plexus when they breathe get by with less than optimal breathing. Shallow breathing limits oxygen intake, which negatively affects blood flow in the body and can create other medical reactions.

In stark contrast to this, breathing techniques can expand oxygen, open the blood flow, and push out toxins. Just as there are many ways to breath, there are many ways to practice intentional breathing exercises. Below is a simple example:

Simple Breathing Technique

1. Be seated in a comfortable chair or on the floor with legs crossed.
2. Slowly, breathe deeply through your nose and expand your abdomen as if it were a balloon, moving to the rib cage and then up to the chest.

3. Then breathe out (exhale) slowly and fully through your mouth or nose as if you were carefully deflating the balloon.
4. Repeat.

The time frame for breathing in can be the same as the time frame for breathing out. For example, you can breathe in for five seconds and out for five seconds. You can also try exhaling twice as long as you inhale. For example, breathe in for five seconds and take ten seconds to breathe out fully. This maximizes the cleansing effect of the exercise.

Do this exercise once or twice a day, perhaps in the morning and at night for at least five minutes.[15] Feel free to experiment with the time spent breathing in and breathing out and with how frequently you do this method. This is a gentle yet powerful practice, so you should never feel dizzy or push yourself. If you begin to feel dizzy or unwell for any reason, stop the session immediately.

While we can do breathing techniques anywhere and anytime— in the car or quickly before a meeting or appointment in a pinch— it generally works best when we are seated comfortably with no distractions. Let it be your time to breathe in and out and focus on the movement of the breath.

The Power of Quality Sleep

A good nights' sleep anchors the day, while
a poor one leaves us rudderless.

Getting a good night's sleep is one of the most important things we can do to heal ourselves. Yet few of us make it a priority, so we walk around half-cocked. Consider the fact that sleep deprivation has been used as a torture technique during wartime to gather intelligence about the enemy. After just two days with no sleep, the prisoners of war began to hallucinate, developed psychosis, and exhibited evidence of cognitive impairment.[16]

While this might be an extreme example of sleep deprivation, the truth is that when we don't get enough sleep every day, even if we're just a couple of hours short, we can experience symptoms similar to prisoners of war. Our ability to function and our body's ability to operate slowly degenerate, severely taxing the mind and body.

The National Sleep Foundation states that sleep is as important to our health and well-being as air, food, and water.[17] When we have a good night's sleep, our bodies and minds regenerate as our bodies support and repair cells, tissues, and the brain. It is a time in which we are unconscious, immobile, and relaxed. Even our breathing and heart rate slows.

A good night's sleep improves cardiovascular health, regulates metabolic and glucose processes, and supports the immune system, which is especially important for anyone fighting illness. Good sleep also supports our emotional health. When we sleep well, we support the mind's ability to retain memory, develop creativity, and rebalance our emotions.[18]

Scientists have learned that during sleep, toxins from the brain are released and sent to the liver for disposal at a quicker rate than when we are awake.[19] The brain also engages in a "consolidation" process of memory in which any unnecessary memories/synapses are removed, such as what your friend had for lunch, while the important ones, such as your upcoming doctor's appointment, are saved.[20]

Quality sleep is vital to healing, the quality of our lives, and even our sense of mental stability. According to the National Institutes of Health, teenagers need at least eight or nine hours of sleep, and adults need seven to nine hours.[21] We are considered cognitively impaired if we get less than six hours, yet it is common for Americans to get only five hours of sleep or less a night. *Cognitively impaired* means we just can't think straight. With just one night of poor sleep, our reaction times slow, so it's easier to get into car accidents; we're less productive; we have trouble remembering things; we get angry more easily; and we just don't enjoy life as much as when we've had a good night's sleep.[22]

Over time, poor sleep can set us up for disease because it creates havoc in the body in many ways. It increases inflammation and weakens the immune system—and, since we interrupt the natural work of sleep, we damage our tissues and impair blood sugar regulation. This makes it easier for us to gain weight and develop diabetes. Poor sleep can also be a risk factor for Alzheimer's disease, obesity, widespread pain, depression, cognitive function, cancer growth, vascular disease, and substance abuse.[23,24]

The good news is that there are many ways to establish healthy and consistently good sleep patterns. The first is to understand your circadian rhythm, also known as the body clock. Every person, animal, and plant, and every tissue in the body, is a part of a circadian rhythm, in which events happen in roughly twenty-four-hour cycles. Our circadian rhythm is influenced by cues from our environment, such as sunlight in the morning, which causes us to wake up, and darkness in the evening, which causes us to feel sleepy.

Circadian rhythms are automatic, but sometimes we go off the program. For example, we get tripped up when we travel and stay in places where the time zone is different than what we are used to. Depending on the depth of the time differential, we feel the effects of jet lag. If we stay in the new environment for a few days, our body clock will ultimately assimilate to the new rhythm.

Connecting to our body clock helps us understand what sleep patterns work best to maximize our health and wellbeing. The body clock gives us cues about when it's time to sleep—as we yawn and feel tired—and when it's time to wake up, among other things. Although our sleep patterns can be different from each other, some being earlier risers and some being night owls, the *timing* of sleep matters.

Our best sleep happens when our circadian rhythm is at its lowest point, which is from ten at night to five in the morning. So, even if we sleep a full eight hours, if we miss much of this key sleep period, the brain, tissues, and cells won't be able to capitalize on their important nighttime work, and we will lose many of the benefits of the sleep cycle.

Alternatively, when we take advantage of the natural rhythms of our sleep patterns, we allow quality sleep to leave us rested and feeling good in the morning. Our mind is fresh, and we feel happier and more able to manage the day's events. Healthier sleep gives us a healthier body, mind, and spirit.

There are many ways to attain regular, beneficial patterns of sleep. In addition to understanding the natural rhythm of the body clock, it's also important to create a calming, relaxed environment at bedtime. Here are some common suggestions for good sleep:

1. Keep a consistent bedtime and wake time.
2. Keep your bedroom cool.
3. Keep your bedroom dark. The darkness helps signal your mind and body that it's time to go to sleep. As you get ready for sleep, you can use a "drift light" that will slowly darken the room over a half-hour time period, encouraging you to feel drowsy and ready to sleep.
4. Ensure there is no noise around you. If you are a light sleeper, you can purchase a sound machine to keep small noises from interrupting your sleep.
5. Keep media and technology out of the bedroom. Turn off all sources of electromagnetic fields (EMFs) in the bedroom, including Wi-Fi, cell phones, tablets, TVs, and any other electrical devices. They are stimulants and can disrupt your circadian rhythm.
6. Make your bedroom a haven—a place to unwind from the stress of the day.
7. Accentuate the differences between night and day by highlighting the natural process of your circadian rhythm. Since the light of morning encourages wakefulness, open the curtains or go outside for a brisk walk when you awaken. Then, when you use your environment to prepare to sleep at night—dim the lights, take a warm bath, create a quiet environment—you give yourself the message that nighttime is a relaxing and restful time. When you become clear about the difference between morning and night, your system has the ability to fall into healthy sleep habits.

8. Avoid alcohol, cigarettes, and caffeine. They are all bad for sleep.
9. If you awaken in the middle of the night and just can't get back to sleep, try the following:

   a. Get out of bed and go to another room.
   b. Keep the lights low.
   c. Do something boring or low-energy—such as reading a magazine or even a children's book with singsong rhythms and calming illustrations—until you feel drowsy again.
   d. Then go back to bed.[25]

The following are a few less-conventional steps to take to support healthy sleep patterns.

Cognitive Therapy

Cognitive therapy helps people reduce their sleep problems. It is based on the idea that when we relax the brain, we relax the body, and that allows us to sleep better. Dr. Jim Otis, functional neurologist and founder of BrainTime.com, believes that consistent sleep problems are a reflection of unhealthy changes in the brain or *negative plasticity.*[26] In other words, the brain is not properly aligned to allow for normal, healthy sleep.

Dr. Otis's patients use earphones and listen to a variety of random beeps in each ear. The beeps help rewire the brain and improve the alignment of the synapses between the right and left brain, allowing for a healthy, natural sleep. I use the technique to help with my sleep, but I also notice additional cognitive benefits, such as general relaxation and sharpened memory.

Chinese Body Clock

In addition to teaching about circadian rhythms, traditional Chinese medicine (TCM) teaches about the association between certain emotions and organs at specific times during the day. For example, if you find yourself waking up several nights in a row at 1:15 a.m., TCM might conclude you are dealing with unresolved anger, rage, or frustration, and that the pattern serves as an alarm clock of sorts, waking you up to the fact that attention is needed.

TCM associates anger with the liver and with the timeframe of one to three in the morning. That's the time when the liver usually does its repair and maintenance, but its ability to do so will be limited if you keep waking up with your unresolved issue about anger. With some awareness of what we experience emotionally, we can sometimes resolve the challenge enough to allow us to resume our natural sleep patterns.

While the dance between the organs and the emotions affect the entire body clock, I only list the common sleep periods here:

Time	Organs	Negative Emotions
9–11 p.m.	thyroid and adrenal glands	hopelessness, confusion, paranoia
11 p.m.–1 a.m.	gall bladder	bitterness, resentment
1–3 a.m.	liver	anger, rage, frustration
3–5 a.m.	lungs	grief, sadness
5–7 a.m.	large intestine	guilt, stuck, defensiveness
7–9 a.m.	stomach	disgust, despair

Some people might be skeptical of this process, but I suggest you try it if you ever get stuck and are sick of staring at your alarm clock night after night. There are many ways to help us resume natural sleep patterns, including the following:

1. **Breathing techniques**—As discussed previously, conscious breathing techniques are a powerful way to help support healthy sleep. When we focus on our breath, we relax our mind and body, which allows us to ease into the sleep process.[27]

2. **Calming oils and salts**—When applied at bedtime, oils such as lavender, sandalwood, and geranium can offer a calming feeling that supports readiness for good sleep. You can use a diffuser or the oil bottle. You can also place the oil on the pressure points on your body, such as the wrist, neck, and head, or massage it onto weary feet and hands. A warm bath with Epsom salts and lavender just before bedtime can also enhance calmness and readiness for healthy slumber.

3. **High-intensity exercise in the morning**—Although exercise is critical to good health, it is best to avoid high-intensity exercise later in the day. Try to exercise in the morning, and perhaps take a light walk after dinner. When we exercise late, we compete with our circadian rhythm, which is preparing for rest. When we buck the system, our body is stimulated, not relaxed, and it may make it harder to get to sleep.

4. **Calming meditation**—Even if it is for just a short period of time, meditation in the morning and evening can help shift your mind away from the thoughts of the day so you are prepared for a good night's sleep.

5. **Melatonin at night to calm**—Our bodies naturally create the hormone melatonin at nighttime to get us ready for sleep. Sometimes taking a melatonin supplement before bedtime can help set the table for the kind of sleep we are looking for. Since it is natural and doesn't make you feel groggy in the morning, as many sleep aids on the market do, it can be a very good choice.

6. **Acupuncture**—TCM believes that acupuncture can be used to release blockages in our life energy and help us enjoy a healthy night's rest.

7. **Guided imagery**—Guided imagery (listening to calming words, sounds, and stories) can be both healing and relaxing.

This can be effective at bedtime to help you more easily drift off to sleep.

8. **Detox**—With proper fasting, we can help push toxins out of the body. The body can resume optimal support, which also helps us find deep sleep.

9. **Eating**—Avoid eating heavy meals three hours before bedtime to allow your system to prepare for sleep instead of waking it up to break down late-night food.

By gaining an awareness of the rhythms of your life, prioritizing sleep, and using some of the suggestions above, you will find that the path to good sleep is well within reach.

Clean Water

Water is essential for life. If we don't drink it, we die. There is no other drink more critical for our bodies than clean H_2O. By drinking plenty of it, we support our brain function, blood flow, and the cells of our bodies, and we get help fighting illnesses by pushing toxins, viruses, and bacteria out.[28] Being hydrated also helps us maintain our body temperature.

Water makes up 60 to 70 percent of your body. For infants, the percentage is even greater. When we don't drink enough water, we become dehydrated, which stresses our systems. Exercising, spending time outside on hot days, and traveling require more water to replenish the body.

Most of us need eight ounces of water eight times per day—or a total of sixty-four ounces—to be our best.[29] If you are busy, it's easy to lose track of how much water you're actually taking in. Some people fill a big container with the amount of clean water they want to drink for the day and keep with them a regular-sized glass for use. It's an easy way to make sure you drink enough water every day.

Taking care of ourselves is not always easy, since many of us live busy lives. However, if you drink clean water instead of beverages like sodas, power drinks, coffee, and juices, you have a better chance of meeting your daily water goal. Generally speaking, store-bought beverages are filled with chemicals and sugars. Coffee is dehydrating, and fruit juices can be considered sugar water if the pulp and fiber have been removed—and they usually are. As a result, these options can't compare to the benefits of clean water when it comes to your health.

In Kelly Turner's excellent book *Radical Remission*, she studied the survivors of serious illness. She explains that the survivors she studied all consider water to be a "master healer."[30] In the book, Turner tells the story of a Japanese man who was diagnosed with advanced kidney cancer and was sent home to die through hospice care. When he came home, he realized that he wanted to drink water, but the tap water he was drinking smelled awful. He started to make good water by using a charcoal carbon filter.

He immediately noticed how much better the clean water tasted, and so he continued to use it. Then he decided to add minerals to the water in an effort to replenish his weak body. Since he was so frail and sick, he couldn't eat anything; the only nutrition he was receiving was through an intravenous tube. In effect, he stumbled onto a way to do a water detox that allowed his organs to rest and repair.

Just because it felt good, he started to venture outside into the sunshine every day. He may not have known it at the time, but the sunshine was giving him healthy doses of vitamin D, an important vitamin. Then, he intuitively found other healing tools that helped him heal. Over time and through his own devices, the man was cured of cancer and was healthy and happy.

While we might know that clean water is essential to good health, and while it might seem simple to drink healthy water, there is a bit of a learning curve about where and how to get the right kind of water to drink. For the most part, we can't rely on tap water, because the processes used by local water plants frequently fail to remove all of the contaminants. Chemicals such as fluoride, chlorine, and heavy metals are commonly in our water sources and can be unsafe and possibly cancer-causing.[31,32] Toxins can also find their way into our water sources through acid rain, agricultural chemicals like pesticides and herbicides, industrial waste run-off, and old pipes that break down metal and plastic.[33]

The crisis in Flint, Michigan, which began in 2014, is a real-life example of the damage that toxins in our water can cause. When people complained of the bad taste, smell, and appearance of the water, government officials assured them that the water was fine. But the water was not fine. In 2016, high levels of lead from old pipes were discovered leaching into the Flint water system. The water had unhealthy levels of heavy metal neurotoxins that made the water unusable and dangerous, especially for children.

I like to believe the Flint, Michigan, water was an unusually bad situation, but you still might want to test your own water through a water-testing kit from a local hardware store or online to be sure you're drinking what you think you're drinking. You can also get your water tested at a state-certified laboratory.

Although it is helpful to know what contaminants may be in your home's water, most of us will need to get a filtered water system of some type anyway. Many grocery stores sell simple handheld filtration systems that typically use an active charcoal filter to remove contaminants in the water. Although these systems remove many impurities, they can't get them all.

Other health-food stores, such as Whole Foods, might offer filtration system ports/dispensers in the water aisle. You can buy a one- to five-gallon empty water container or bring one from home and fill it up from one of the clean water choices they offer, such as reverse osmosis water. RO is a system that uses a semipermeable membrane to remove impurities in water.

Another option is to rent or own a glass or plastic BPA-free watercooler filled with spring water—for example, at your home or business. Locate a reputable water delivery service in your area.

The best solution might be to buy and install a home filtration system with reverse osmosis and/or active carbon filtration. These systems connect to your home water source. Some can be simply installed under your kitchen sink or on your counter. More sophisticated systems can purify all the water in your home, including the shower. Although this may be one of the best solutions, it is usually one of the most expensive, too.

As most of us are mobile, our water must be mobile as well. The best materials for water containers are glass, ceramic, and stainless steel. The next best choices are plastic bottles that are BPA-free. Plastic bottles that are not in one of these categories might have been made with BPA, or bisphenol A, which is a chemical used in some plastics that might be connected to cancer. The chemical toxins in the plastic can leach into the drinking water.

Adding a little bit of squeezed lemon juice to your drinking water can be beneficial, since it is a natural cleanser. It helps the digestive system and the immune system, and it adds vitamin B, vitamin C, and magnesium. You can squeeze other kinds of fruit juice, and even a little bit of pink Himalayan sea salt, into your water for extra minerals and taste.

Dive into the world of clean water and see what happens. Once you have the basics, it's simple and just requires your commitment to keep your body filled with this good stuff.

Exercise

When we exercise on a regular basis, it doesn't only feel good and help us feel more energetic, it also strengthens the body and supports health, vitality, and the ability to fight, and even cure, certain illnesses. It can also be a lot of fun.

One of the reasons exercising is important for health and healing is that when we exercise, we use more oxygen-improving circulation, which supports our muscles, lungs, and heart. The energy that is created from this process is critical for our cells, tissues, and organs to work properly.

Our cells are the basic building blocks of our bodies, so when they are oxygenated—for example, from regular exercise—the natural metabolic processes of the body are optimized, and we can thrive as a result. This includes fighting cancer cells, removing toxins, digesting bacteria, and making cellular repairs.

We can experience the benefits of exercise directly in other ways, too: through the reduction of unwanted weight and inflammation, better digestion, improved appearance of our skin, improved memory and clarity, creation of feel-good hormones called endorphins, and improved sleep.

If this isn't enough good news, when we exercise consistently, our bodies become more responsive to the activity. This makes it easier for our muscles to take in oxygen, which creates even more energy to heal us.

A hundred years ago, people were much more active than we are today with all of our conveniences. Although society has shifted to a more sedentary lifestyle, it doesn't change the fact that, on a cellular level, we were built to be active. That was the bargain: we move, and the cells do their thing. Don't move, and the cells will break down and, ultimately, the physical body will break down more quickly too.

Because it's clear that exercise is good for us and adopting a permanent healthy exercise program makes sense, it's important to find a way to make it satisfying and even enjoyable. It's a good idea to mix activities to make things more interesting and to exercise different parts of your body. Some people like to work out by themselves, while others prefer to exercise in groups. There are lots of ways to do this.

Here are some exercise ideas:

- brisk walking—outside (neighborhood, park, school track) or inside (mall, treadmill)
- running—outside (neighborhood, park, school track) or inside (treadmill)
- bike riding, outside or inside (stationary bike)
- elliptical—like a treadmill, but easier on feet, knees and legs
- hiking
- dancing classes
- exercise classes
- basketball

- joining a gym and going
- jump rope
- yoga
- swimming
- free weights
- stomach crunches
- jumping jacks
- climbing flights of stairs
- stretching
- rebounding (personal trampoline)
- tai chi/qigong

To get the best results, work out like you mean it. Reading *War and Peace* on the stationary bike is probably not going to cut it. Focus on your body, feel the experience, and connect to it. You can learn a lot that way.

Generally, to maximize the benefits of consistent exercise, the goal is to work out for about thirty minutes to an hour, at least four or five days a week, subject to your doctor's approval. It's important to know your limitations and to consult your doctor anytime you begin a new physical program, especially if you have a medical condition.

That being said, if you are just starting to exercise, it's a good idea to start slowly. Even walking for ten minutes a day for a week, increasing the time every week thereafter up to thirty minutes regularly, can put you on the right path.

No matter what the activity or its duration, the key will be to maintain a regular routine. Morning time is usually more reliable than afternoons or evenings for exercising, since the latter option can often get derailed by the day. It is also important to increase the amount of clean water you drink during and after workouts in order to replenish your body and push out toxins.

Exercise is an integral, vital aspect of living a happy and healthy life—it is a gift every time. So when you work out, imagine your cells cheering for you, and your mind and spirit doing the same. Have fun!

Chapter 4

More About the Body

Quality nutrition and managing toxins support our body just like breathing techniques, quality sleep, clean water and exercise. We eat food all the time yet so many of us are unaware of what we are actually ingesting and how it might be affecting us negatively. It's the same situation with toxins in our environment. Having a better understanding of these challenges, and making better choices, improve our ability to support our health and our bodies more optimally.

Nutrition Doesn't Have to Be Boring

Most automobiles run on gas, just as humans run on food and water. If you fill your car's fuel tank with the wrong kind of gas, the car won't work well and will ultimately stop working completely. It's the same with us. The nutrients we take in feed our cells, our internal organs, our brain, and even our mood. Poor-quality food is poor fuel for your body, while high-quality food, especially natural, live food, offers better fuel for your body to use.

I knew a man who only ate one time a day: dinnertime. When he did eat, he didn't consume healthy foods, choosing burgers instead of vegetables and fruit. Although his eating habits contributed to many surgeries to remove painful gallbladder stones, he refused to change the way he was eating. He chose to ignore the connection between his diet and his body.

I once spoke to a group of people in various stages of brain cancer and encountered another person with a similar attitude. I was sharing my story and explaining what I had learned about self-healing, and when I started talking about healthy foods and the specific foods we should avoid, a man in the audience yelled out that he was not going to change a thing about his diet because, he said, "We do need a quality of life, you know!" At that, he marched over to a table with cookies, took a handful, and marched back to his seat, taking a defiant stance.

I was surprised by what he said, but I respected it, too. Everyone is different, and we each have our own individual path. But if your path is to avoid illness or fight illness, it is important to incorporate a healthy diet.

When we make nutrition a priority, we allow our mind and body to flourish. When we fill our bodies with junk food and processed foods that are high in calories, sugar, chemicals, and salt, it is harder for the body to run well. Over time, the poor fuel becomes too much for our overtaxed body, and problems start creeping in, such as inflammation, illness, weight gain, high blood pressure, heart issues, some cancers, and type 2 diabetes—to name just a few.

The food we eat either helps our body or it doesn't. If you're fighting an illness, it makes sense to fuel your body with nutrients that support it instead of those that can knock it down. Even if you are not dealing with illness but you realize that food is a key component of staying healthy, it is important to learn at least the basics. Here, the goal is to simply point you in a direction that might open your eyes to improved health through good nutrition.

Food as Medicine

Before I started my healing journey, I thought I had a good working understanding of nutrition. I thought I ate well. I had been essentially a vegetarian for years (although I did eat fish). Yet I got sick. When I started to learn more about nutrition, I became disgusted by the food that ends up in our grocery stores and in our mouths.

Processed foods, chemicals, pesticides, and the ridiculous amount of sugar that is added to our food are making us sick—or worse.

More than 73 percent of Americans are overweight or obese.[34] It's not too surprising, since our country also wins the dubious award of leading all countries in per capita sugar consumption.[35] As a result, more than 42 percent of all Americans are considered obese[36] yet many *malnourished*—partly because they are consuming plenty of poor-quality calories that provide little or no nutritional value. This deadly trend, which has been growing consistently over the past two decades, is dramatically and negatively affecting our health.

These *nonfoods*, as I call them, which are stripped of their natural nutritional value, usually include plenty of refined sugars, refined flour, chemicals, additives, and preservatives. The food companies do what they can to make the food taste good and to extend the shelf life of their products in order to maximize profits. Do you really want to eat anything that will still be edible in two years?

What should be a great concern for everyone is the connection between cancer and the amount of processed sugar in American food. A cancer cell can absorb significantly more sugar than a normal healthy cell. Cancer cells thrive on sugar—in fact, they depend on it. Although we don't want to feed the cancer cells, the problem is that we actually need sugar to survive. The good news is that not all sugars are equal in quality and benefit. Processed or refined sugar is the worst type of sugar.

When we eat processed sugars, such as those in cookies, our blood sugar level spikes, and we often experience a temporary sugar high. It can also be the beginning of an inflammatory reaction in the body. After the high, our blood sugar level crashes, and we feel famished—often reaching for the same offending processed food (like the rest of the cookies in the box). Yet that will not give the body what it really needs—nourishment.

In such a state, the body's systems are not in balance, and the body is confused about whether or not it is hungry. While your body craves more food, your brain knows you have eaten recently. But when we eat whole foods instead of processed foods, the craving dynamic goes away. The fiber and the quality of the food slow the process, allowing the body to absorb the nutrients and providing that full feeling. Drama ended.

Big swings in blood sugar levels are harmful, especially when you're fighting cancer. They can create inflammation, weaken the immune system, and destabilize the body, giving cancer cells easier access. When you allow your body to go through the ups and downs of the roller-coaster ride of blood sugar levels, it is forced to focus its energy on the irregularities in the bloodstream instead of the important task of fighting cancer. It's the same when we don't have cancer—the body is still being derailed to deal with the self-imposed irritation and inflammation in the body due to our food choices. Why weaken your body with foods that don't serve you well?

Fruits and vegetables are good choices for sugars, as they are natural and include vital nutrients and fiber. Healthy foods fuel the body much better than processed foods do. In addition to fruits and vegetables, a healthy diet will include a variety of foods, such as beans, nuts, fish, and healthy fats. When we eat a balanced diet of natural, live foods like these, we give ourselves the best chance to promote maximum health.

Getting Started

The best way to get started with eating well is to dive into your pantry and throw everything away that is processed and expired. You might need to get a big garbage bag for this purging. I've provided several lists in the back of the book to help guide your pantry removal as well as your journey to the grocery store. Appendix A offers a beginner's guide to healthy food. Appendix B helps you decide when to choose organic. Appendix C reveals the food additives you need to avoid from now on. Appendix D will enlighten you about sneaky sugars.

When you go to the grocery store, be sure to carefully investigate the ingredients of a product you are considering. The fewer ingredients, the better. These days, if I see a product with more than five ingredients listed, especially if they are filled with long words that are hard to read or say out loud, I don't even consider it as an option.

A word of caution: the marketing departments of companies that produce processed foods will make unbelievable promises like "wholesome" and "healthy for you." Do not believe it. You need to read the actual ingredients and research it if you still don't understand it. It is the only thing we can do to counteract their slick advertising.

As many customers are getting more savvy about limiting processed sugar content, there's a new game in town. The food companies are hiding processed sugars under different names in the ingredients. This makes it harder for us to understand which sugars were added to the product. Bring my list of sneaky sugars (appendix D) to the grocery store to help you.

Whatever the food is, remember that the goal is to find healthier alternatives that will allow you to thrive and feel better. Common side effects of healthy eating include more energy, reduced inflammation, improved health, better sleep, losing weight naturally, clear skin, improved mood, and generally feeling happier.

There's a lot to learn about nutrition and healthy food, but don't let it overwhelm you. We all have to start somewhere, and you will thank yourself many times over once you get the hang of it. This kind of eating is *not* a diet. It is a permanent life change.

In addition to the appendices mentioned in this section, you'll find helpful books and resources, including recipe books and my favorite magazine dedicated to healthy food, in appendix F.

Incorporating Herbs and Spices

Herbs and spices haven't only provided us with pleasant, tasty additions to the foods we eat and drink; they have been used for healing virtually since the beginning of recorded history. Herbs were used in Mesopotamia in 5000 BC, and in India, China, and Egypt thousands of years ago as well. Ancient Greeks and Romans used herbs and spices for healing, as did people in the Middle Ages. It wasn't until the early 1900s that medical professionals became enticed by synthetic chemical compounds and eschewed the historical uses of herbs and spices.

Fortunately, there has been a resurgence of interest in the health benefits of herbs and spices in recent years. They can be used to strengthen the immune system and lower blood sugar and cholesterol, and they can have anti-inflammatory benefits. My list of favorites starts with turmeric (curcumin). Turmeric is at its most potent in liquid or capsule form for anti-inflammation benefits, and it is often used with additives like black pepper extract to boost absorption. But the root (after you remove the rough outer skin) can be chopped and added to meals, soups, and even smoothies for our benefit.

Ginger is known to help fight nausea and prevent stomach upset. It's also a powerful antioxidant. You can actually suck on it (but skin it first) and add it to your smoothie or to tea, meals, and soups to get the benefits. You can also find it in supplement form.

Garlic is a favorite for many, as it tastes great, but it also has been shown to lower cancer risk and might also provide cardiovascular support. You can cook your meals with garlic, and you can buy it in supplement form as well.

Rosemary has antioxidant properties and can be added to your meals or taken in extract form. Similarly, licorice tastes good and inhibits inflammation.

One of the things I like most about incorporating herbs and spices in my food is that we can grow the plants ourselves. Basil (uplifting, antibacterial, anti-inflammatory), oregano (antifungal, immune stimulant), chamomile (helps relax us), lemon balm (fights viruses), and peppermint (can invigorate and uplift us) are just a few herbs that are easily grown at home.

I encourage you to experiment with various herbs and spices as you improve your nutrient profile. You can transform the foods you eat by incorporating these natural helpers. There are many comprehensive books dedicated to this topic. One good source, the Herbal Drugstore, is listed in the back of this book.

Understanding Acidic and Alkaline Foods

One of the most important things to know about cancer cells is that they thrive best in an acidic environment in the body. On the other hand, an alkaline environment generally works in the opposite way—it is like kryptonite to cancer cells.

The reason is that an alkaline diet helps balance the pH levels in the body, supports essential minerals, and promotes higher levels of oxygen, too, giving critical support to our organs, cells and immune system. In contrast, overly acidic body tissues can be a contributing factor for cancer growth[37] by supporting inflammation and low oxygenation in the body.[38]

As a result, the food we choose should include a balance between alkaline-forming foods and acid-forming foods, with an emphasis on alkaline-forming foods to maximize health. Whether we are fighting cancer or not, an alkaline environment more easily allows the body to fight abnormal cells lurking in our bodies. Here, the environment better supports oxygenation and the immune system's ability to identify cell abnormalities and destroy them much better than an acidic one could.

It is notable that if the immune system is unable to stop a cancer cell, the cancer cell can switch to an anaerobic state, as mentioned earlier in the breathing section. In this state the cancer cell no longer relies on oxygen but, instead, on glucose (sugar) to thrive. Even so, supporting an alkaline environment might not only help fight against cancer cells and potential cancer cells but also slow down the rate of cancer growth in the body.[39]

It's also important to note that emotional stress can foster an acidic environment in the body. Troublemakers such as processed foods, sugar, and excessive animal products also help to feed acidic conditions. Over time, those conditions make it harder for the body to absorb minerals and nutrients and can compromise the cells' ability to create energy, repair themselves, and flush toxins.

To establish a more alkaline environment in our bodies, we can eat most vegetables, olive oil, some nuts, herbal teas, and some fruits, such as lemons, watermelon, and grapefruit. The challenge is to learn which foods are alkaline and which are acidic—it's not always obvious. For example, although almonds and cashews are alkaline-forming foods, walnuts are acidifying.

For optimal health, it's not necessary to exclude acidic foods completely. In fact, that would not give you the balance you are looking for. The key is to incorporate both acidic foods and alkaline foods while favoring the alkaline ones. (For a brief look at which foods are acidic and which are alkaline, see appendix E.)

Testing your pH level will help you understand if your body tends to be more acidic or alkaline. You will need pH strips (pH 5.5 to 8.0), which you can purchase online, at a pharmacy, or at a clinical nutritionist's office. To take the test, simply rip off a strip and either put it on your tongue for the saliva test or in your urine stream.

I have seen optimal pH urine target ranges from 6.2 in the morning to 7.4 at night, but I have seen other ranges as well. Similarly, I have seen optimal saliva values range from 6.8 in the morning to 7.2 at night, with variations from other sources. Either way, look for results in the green range—not the yellow colors that indicate an acidic environment. There is a range, so we don't want it to be too low or too high to get the maximum benefit.

Some people drink a big glass of water and add a teaspoon or so of regular baking soda each day to support the alkaline environment in addition to focusing on alkaline-forming foods. You can also take supplements like calcium, magnesium, and vitamin D to support an alkaline environment, especially if you are fighting cancer.[40]

Earlier in this book, we discussed the importance of oxygen and carbon dioxide with respect to exercise and breathing techniques. Similarly, the oxygen created in a more alkaline diet is yet another example of choices we can make that improve the body's ability to work at its optimal level.

The Benefits of Supplements

It would be nice to think that if we ate well, we wouldn't need supplements. But the reality is that it is very hard to get all the nutrients we need even if we are eating very well. Part of the problem is that the quality of the soil that helps grow our food isn't as good as the soil was a hundred years ago. Erosion, for one, has helped create nutrient-depleted soil.

Pesticides, overseeding, and overgrowing have also weakened the minerals and nutritional quality of many farmed foods. No one can argue that the typical tomatoes we buy at the grocery can't compare to home-grown tomatoes. The lackluster tomatoes from the grocery store taste weak, and it's likely they're not as nutritious as home-grown tomatoes or those grown a hundred years ago. And so it goes with a lot of our food—not just the tomatoes.

The right supplements can help enhance the immune system, reduce inflammation, and strengthen our systems in other ways so that we are healthier and stronger. While they can be valuable for maintaining general good health, they are especially important when our systems are compromised and faltering, as when we are fighting illness. In such situations, the use of supplements can be crucial.

In my case, once I was diagnosed, I immediately located an experienced integrative medicine doctor. Even before my surgery, she began giving me supplements to help fight the inflammation and strengthen the immune system, which is critical when fighting illness.

The doctor handling my radiation seemed particularly concerned about the supplements. He explained that some of them are so potent and effective that they can counteract the work of the radiation—which is a powerful treatment in and of itself, as it is designed to kill cells, good and bad. As a result, my integrative doctor took me off of certain supplements during that time so the radiation would not be negatively affected.

I thought that the concern of the radiation doctor was very telling, but I was a little confused when a couple of the oncologists I worked with didn't seem to care whether I took supplements or not, saying, "If it makes you feel good, go ahead."

Regardless of the mixed messages, I concluded that if supplements can be a threat to radiation, there must be something to them. To bolster this position, I want to tell you about my friend who was diagnosed with incurable stage 4 non-Hodgkin's lymphoma with a very poor prognosis. His doctors gave him five years to live.

My friend took control of his diagnosis, and through his research, he discovered the benefits of certain supplements. He found an experienced chiropractic doctor who had been focusing on nutrition and supplements for over twenty years with very good results. My friend started taking a variety of supplements in addition to eating clean food and staying relaxed by using meditation to limit inflammation in his body.

By the end of the year, he had achieved a complete remission from his disease. He stopped his chemotherapy treatment midcourse. The doctors were shocked. My friend tried to tell them about his protocol and his use of supplements, but they had no interest in it and just chalked it up to luck. How frustrating.

Regardless, my friend has well eclipsed the expectations of his doctors and is now free of cancer. Like me, he continues his healing protocols because he knows they work for him.

You can buy supplements at specialty nutrition stores and some quality grocery stores, such as Whole Foods. Ask for a specialist in the store to help you navigate the products and their benefits. You can also search online so long as you research the company and the quality of its supplements. I have had the best luck buying the right supplements for me through naturopaths, clinical nutritionists (many of whom are chiropractors), and integrative medical doctors.

Since everyone has different needs, it is helpful to at least start with a good specialist who will know how to use live food and supplements to help your healing process. A specialist can create a list of supplements tailored to your needs, as well as support your other nutritional issues. And, since all supplements are not equal in quality, an experienced professional can help guide you to make better-quality choices.

One of the things I learned through this process was to break down my daily supplements throughout the day (maybe at each meal) to maximize the nutritional benefit of absorption. This practice limits the marvel of bright colors emanating from the toilet, thereby flushing away much of the benefits.

If you choose to go it alone, I suggest you get a good book about supplements to guide you. There are many of them. Just make sure you get quality supplements and the right ones to support you best.

Regardless of where you decide to get your supplements, be careful of what I call "supplement creep." As you start feeling better due to taking supplements and, hopefully, all the other good things you are doing for yourself, it is very possible to continue to add new supplements without removing from your list any of the existing ones. As a result, you can end up taking a lot of supplements and probably more than you need. It's up to you to manage the number of supplements you want to take.

Detoxification and Avoiding Toxins

No matter how much we try to drink the cleanest water or eat the purest fruits and vegetables, there are always toxins lurking in and around our bodies. They are in our food, our skin, our breath, our homes, and our workplaces. They are in the grass we walk on and the water we drink. Unless we live in a bubble, there is no way to avoid all of the toxins that exist in our lives. That's why it is so important to be aware of toxins, to avoid them when possible, and to detoxify them when we can't.

People have been practicing detoxing for a very long time. Detoxification is an essential aspect of Ayurveda, a traditional healing system in India and one of the oldest forms of medicine in the world. A tenet of another ancient system, Traditional Chinese Medicine, is that toxins must be removed from the body because they block energy flow and can damage our health. Many ancient cultures practiced detoxifying the body. For instance, Native Americans had sweat lodges, the ancient Greeks and Romans were famous for their baths, and people in Nordic countries like Finland have a longstanding practice using saunas.[41]

We are part of an ongoing history of people who've been aware and concerned about toxins in the body and who've had systems to remove them for health purposes. Although the toxins in our current world may be different from those thousands of years ago, they are still of great concern.

There are many sources of toxins in our lives. For example, many types of electromagnetic energy—including microwaves, microwave towers, cell phones, cordless phones, laptops, and Wi-Fi, can be damaging to our health. They emit various levels of electromagnetic fields that interact with our bodies in ways most of us aren't aware of.

I am especially interested in the connection between mobile phones and brain cancer. Many of the brain cancer survivors I have met confirmed that the side of the head they used to talk on their cell phone was the same area in which the brain cancer emerged. That was certainly the case with me—and I used it a lot.

Infamously, Johnny Cochran, one of the lead lawyers defending O. J. Simpson in his first trial for murder, died of brain cancer. All accounts were that, being a busy lawyer, he constantly held his phone against his head—the same location where the brain cancer showed up. It doesn't take a rocket scientist to figure out that placing a hot battery against your head (or any other part of your body) for an extended period of time is probably not so good for your health.

Mobile and cordless phones both affect the brain, as they emit radio-frequency (RF) radiation where the device is being used. In May 2011, the International Agency for Research on Cancer (IARC) at the World Health Organization[42] provided an "evaluation of scientific evidence" regarding brain tumor risk and RF radiation.

The IARC observed links between RF radiation—from mobile phones, base stations, Wi-Fi access points, smartphones, laptops, and tablets—and the head and brain, and specifically to glioma and acoustic neuroma, which are forms of brain tumors. Their conclusion was that, at certain frequency ranges, the devices are considered a "possible" human carcinogen (Classification-Group 2B). The WHO offered these protective steps:

> A person using a mobile phone 30-40 cm [roughly, 11-15 inches] away from their body, for example when text messaging, accessing the Internet or using a "hand-free" device, will therefore have a much lower exposure to radiofrequency fields than someone holding the handset against their head.[43]

Basically, radiofrequency radiation affects us in a negative way. For some, it might be a lot, and for others, it might be minimal. While scientists study this area further, it is clear to me that at least it's in our best interest to reduce the toxic load of RF radiation however we can. Remember, we are the guinea pigs in the experiment, not unlike those who smoked cigarettes in the early days. And we know how that ended up. We would be wise to come to our own conclusions when dealing with these potential carcinogens.

Just as we need to be careful with our devices, we also need to be aware of other toxins around us, in our homes, and in our workplace. Our skin, for example, is our largest organ, and when we use chemicals on our face, on our hands, and in our hair, we potentially add to our toxic load. Chemicals such as coal tar, parabens, lead, formaldehyde, sodium lauryl sulfate, and fragrances are just a few of the worrisome ingredients that end up on our skin and hair. That's why it's important to choose "clean" quality products (like good-quality food) for our health's sake.

It's also important to note that alcohol, illegal drugs, overuse of legal drugs, cigarettes, and vaping are serious blows to our health and should be avoided. When it comes to alcohol intake in particular— the most socially acceptable drug for most people—the stomach, blood system, tissues, liver, and ultimately the brain (which takes the brunt of it) are flooded with it, creating inflammation, weakening our immune system, and negatively affecting the brain's communication pathways. Obviously, alcohol is a popular drink, so perhaps the better message is about moderation for those who are well and healthy. But for those fighting illness, alcohol shouldn't be an option if your goal is to heal.

Regardless of where these toxins come from, there are ways to minimize their harmful effects. The first step is to be knowledgeable about the threats. The second is to avoid as many toxins as possible. Third, it's helpful to detoxify.

There are many ways to detoxify the body. One is to refrain or severely limit eating for a day or so as you flood the body with plenty of clean water, thereby pushing out toxins. This practice also gives your organs a respite from the constant need to break down food and beverages, thereby giving the body time to repair. It's not unlike a road being closed for repairs. To restore it, drivers don't use it for a while.

When you limit food intake temporarily, the liver can focus on detoxification, helping to push toxins through the kidneys for removal from the body. Even one day of doing this can help expel some of the buildup. Don't be surprised if you start feeling a little bad during this process, especially when you do it for the first time. Old toxins are being dredged up for removal, and that can make you feel not so hot for a little while.

Once the body has had the opportunity to dredge things out, you can start feeling better. This is one of the reasons why drinking plenty of water helps remove toxins. A successful detox cleansing should leave you feeling great, full of energy, and able to sleep much better.

If you are considering a detox of any kind, be sure to talk with your doctor first. Also, as there are so many ways to do it, be sure to consult a reputable source—perhaps a naturopath or integrative medical doctor, for example—so you find the right and healthiest protocol for you.

Understanding the risks of some of the common toxins around us, in us, and on us can help to repel unwanted chemicals and radiation. That's something worth doing for all of us.

Chapter 5

The Mind: Moving Energy to Heal

The moment a person chooses to move their own energy, they awaken the healer within them.
—*Qigong Master Chunyi Lin*

Energy is everywhere, whether we are aware of it or not. We are all energetic beings, and we sense other people's energy, too. Consider these common comments:

- "I have a funny feeling about her."
- "I just have a hunch about this."
- "I don't like his energy."
- "I love his energy."
- "I got a weird feeling/vibe from her."
- "I feel it in my gut."
- "I love being around her. She is an old soul."

We have the power to understand energy, but sometimes we lose our energetic radar—our confidence in our natural instincts. The practice of mindfulness helps us find our radar again. It can support our wellness by helping us understand ourselves more deeply, along with what we really need emotionally, and it reminds us how to nurture ourselves and pay attention to where we are and what we think about that.

The tools discussed in this section can help you harness your mind and support your body by quieting and adjusting your thoughts. Doing so can build personal creativity, allowing you to feel freer and more authentic. You can learn about, apply, and *feel* the power of music, visualization, qigong, meditation, joy, and so much more.

Although most of these tools are not complicated to understand or use, they can be impactful no matter where you are in your healing journey. And you just might love what you find. Let's dive in!

Qigong

Qigong is a simple yet powerful technique originating in China more than 2,000 years ago. The practice is a combination of gentle body movements and deep breathing. Although it might work best done standing up, if you are not feeling well enough to stand, it can also be surprisingly effective in a seated position.

The practice of qigong allows us to move energy and clear the mind. People typically feel safe, well, and very calm while doing qigong exercises—feelings that often extend well beyond the practice. My fingers tingle when I have finished doing qigong, so much so that my dog hangs around me, waiting to get extra rubs with my energized hands.

Part of the reason qigong feels so good is that it helps us unwind our energy. Like unkinking a garden hose, qigong releases the *qi* (our energy source) and helps it to flow like water. As a result, it's possible to feel strong emotions when doing qigong. As the water in the garden hose freely flows, so can our blocked emotions, including gratitude, sadness, and joy. It can be surprising when our emotions catch up to us and we see a window into our inner truth that we didn't know was there before. It is a gift.

Other gifts arrive when we experience a new perspective we'd never considered before. Sometimes we might just find ourselves with a simple wide smile for no reason at all. To get the best results of practicing qigong, quiet your mind while doing the qigong movements.

One of the reasons qigong is impactful for so many people, and especially for those fighting cancer and other illnesses, is that when we free our qi to circulate, the mind, body, and spirit have the opportunity to be in balance, as it is meant to be. The flow of the qi calms our whole system, sending messages of healing and wellness throughout the body and creating more energy to fight illness.

In this way, the following systems of the body are positively affected:

1. **Circulation**—Circulation allows for a more alkaline environment in the body rather than an acidic one. As described earlier, an acidic pH environment supports cancer growth, but an alkaline one does not.
2. **Respiratory system**—An oxygenated environment improves the immune system, which fights cancer and all disease.
3. **Autonomic system**—Qigong allows us to unwind and feel relaxed, which, in turn, supports many aspects of our health, including the immune system and our sense of wellness. When we are calm and balanced, natural healing can more readily take place.

Qigong is easier to teach visually than with the written word. You can find many websites and demonstrations of it online. For example, you'll find Lee Holden, a well-known qigong instructor who has been featured on network television many times, teaching qigong. I also have a special place in my heart for Chunyi Lin, a qigong master, teacher, and speaker. You can learn about him on his website at www.springforestqigong.com. I used his *SFQ-Level One for Health with Master Chunyi Lin* every day for more than two years to help me in my fight against cancer. These are just two suggestions to get you started.

Although I had never heard of qigong before I got sick, it became one of the most important tools I used to keep me relaxed, improve my mood, and help me feel unbelievably well while I was ill—and even now, when I am well. You might be surprised how adding this to your toolbox can make such a difference in your life. It just might become one of your favorites too.

Meditation

Meditation is a way to quiet the mind, allow healing, and inspire connection. One way to think about meditation is that it is a way to reclaim space in your mind with focused relaxation. Even though it's conceptually pretty simple to do, it's not always easy. Our minds are constantly hopping from one thought to another—some refer to it as *monkey mind*. Most of us don't even realize how much we do it. Taking time to meditate allows you to slow down the banter and, sometimes temporarily, quiet it completely.

Even if it's just for a while, meditation can create a sense of relief and then space, clarity, and relaxation. The body takes these cues to help improve our brain function, nervous system, and immune system, among other healthy benefits.

As with any new skill, the more you practice, the easier it is to do, and the better your results get. After meditation, many people feel calmer, more grounded, and wiser somehow. Occasionally, you may be surprised to receive wisdom or clarity concerning something in your life. When we meditate, we ask for nothing and give nothing. The practice is freeing to the mind, allowing us to simply exist.

To begin to meditate, find a calming and quiet environment with the lights low. You might want to add a candle or some pleasant-smelling oils to enhance the space you are creating. Once there, sit down cross-legged, if possible. If that position is not comfortable, find a different sitting position that works for you.

Close your eyes to shut out the busyness of the world. Begin to breathe deeply and gently in and out in a rhythmic manner, while continuing your focus on the breath through the meditation. After a few moments, you will start to settle down. Try not to think about anything. This is normally where the monkey mind hops in. Don't beat yourself up for wandering; just simply and gently redirect yourself to the quiet mind of the meditation. Over time, it will be easier to control the thoughts that seep in.

Some people begin the practice of meditation by doing it for five minutes in the morning and five minutes at night before bed. Over time, you might meditate for twenty to thirty minutes once or twice a day. But there are no steadfast rules except that going beyond thirty minutes might be too long for most people. Experiment with what works best for you.

Guided Meditation

Guided meditation has been called the "lazy man's meditation" because all we need to do is close our eyes and listen to the words and the music to get the benefits. We are introduced to calming sounds and a speaker who gently brings us along on a journey of vibrant images and positive thoughts. Imagine your mind being massaged by a crystal-clear ocean sending healing messages to your thoughts. It's so easy, yet it can be very impactful.

As the listener, your only job is to create a private, quiet location in which you can lie down, try to keep your mind clear, and listen to the music and the healing words. It's possible to doze off because you feel so calm, safe, and relaxed. (Don't listen to these meditations while driving a car.) When you are done, you may have the sense that you have shifted some of your thoughts, feelings, and perspectives for the better. The continual use of guided meditation makes that feeling even stronger.

My favorite guided meditation CDs are from Belleruth Naparstek at healthjourneys.com. Naparstek pioneered guided imagery. Several studies have reported healing effects for people who listen to her meditations. One of the studies showed that patients using Naparstek's calming tapes did better during surgery and recovery than those who did not use the tapes. The results showed that those using the tapes lost less blood during surgery and, on average, left the hospital a full day earlier than the control group.[44]

Subsequent studies have shown that guided imagery helps the immune system, improves blood pressure, and minimizes allergic reactions. It can also help reduce pain, depression, anxiety, and phobias.[45] Generally, directed meditation can calm the nervous system and allow the body to return to homeostasis or balance. In turn, the body can release the fight/flight response and get back to the business of fighting illness and keeping the body healthy and well.

There are many choices for buying guided meditation CDs online, as well as through apps like the Calm app, or at your local holistic New Age store. It can be a great gift for someone in need, including yourself.

Prayer

For some people, prayer offers the highest level of connection to God and connection to the purpose of our lives here on earth. Many experience solace through prayer. There are many ways to pray; it can be as simple as crying out, "*Help!*"

Here is a sequence I like, which consists of three steps:

1. Warm up with gratitude.

> *I am grateful for the sun and the moon and the sunshine on my face. I am grateful for my family and my friends. I am grateful for my resilience. Thank You. I am grateful for those who pull me up when I feel down. How grateful I am for those people in my life who make me laugh. Thank you for my laughter. How grateful I am to be alive. Even though I might often miss the mark, I am grateful to have the opportunity to do better tomorrow and grow my spirit bigger and better than yesterday. Thank you for these blessings.*

Praying this way, or with your personal version that seems right for you, gives you a chance to catalog all the riches—often simple ones—in your life instead of focusing on the things you don't have or what you don't want in your life. This is a powerful way to reaffirm the good in your life, no matter how small it may be.

2. Pray for others.

> *I pray for healing of the trouble in my friend's life and his concern about his [health/marriage/ problem]. Please support him. Let him find the path and the way to help his challenge. I pray for his wisdom-I pray you will show him the way. I pray for his peace.*

It is helpful to use your energy as a gift to someone in your family, to a friend, or to anyone else in need. This kind of giving can be powerful medicine for your spirit—in addition to the recipient's—by realizing that other people are also in need, not just you. In so doing, you reclaim power for yourself.

3. Pray for yourself

> *God, I pray that I am more patient when I react to things in my life. I pray for more joy than frustration. I pray for light, wisdom, calm, and peace. May the love of God be within me. Please support me in my hopes, dreams, and challenges. Help me find the strength and grace to manage my daily walk in life. I pray for your infinite light and love around me and within me. I know that all things are possible through you, and I am grateful.*

When we pray for ourselves, we privately pray for whatever is in our hearts. Anything at all; it is between you and the Creator. No matter where you are, you are praying in your private sanctuary, and there are no secrets there.

There is no right or wrong way to pray. The examples above are merely ideas that might help you create your own inspired prayers. Avoid saying words that don't mean anything to you, because your ability to access a higher level can't be faked. The only rule is to be yourself and be painfully honest about your true thoughts. This is how you can create a conversation with higher levels of consciousness, love, and energy.

Visualization

Visualization is a technique that helps us to focus on an inspired outcome. We can visualize anything, from an anticipated interview or business event to an upcoming athletic performance, or even our health. The reason visualization can effect real change is that the mind and the body are intimately connected. When you focus your mind on detailed, specific steps to your desired result, the body can follow in kind and manifest what you want.

Many athletes use visualization to help manifest their chosen goals. One of my favorite examples is the story of Novak Djokovic, one of the best tennis players in the world. In his book *Serve to Win*, he discusses his life growing up in wartime Belgrade, Serbia, and how he learned to adapt and keep an open mind. This experience allowed him to learn and use visualization in preparation for his matches. "I believe that there is a law of attraction: you get the things that you produce in your thoughts," he has said.[46]

Similarly, Carli Lloyd, a member of the US women's soccer team that won the World Cup in 2015, describes her use of visualization to achieve what she wants. For her team's historic win, she visualized scoring goals. Over and over, she saw herself doing it. She scored three that day, in fact, and was the first woman in World Cup history to do so.

These are just two examples of how many athletes harness the power of the mind and the body to achieve incredible results. Visualization can affect health challenges in much the same way.

When we apply visualization techniques to help with illness or injury, we allow ourselves to relax our nervous system and improve breathing. This helps to support, even stimulate, the immune system that fights illness and facilitates healing.[47] The idea is that the mind can influence the immune system. And the more we support the immune system, the more we support health.

As a result, the more we allow ourselves to believe and "see" the visualization as if it were true, the more we reinforce the message, allowing the body to also believe it is true. When we have nightmares, sometimes we wake up drenched in sweat, with hands clenched and heart pounding. In our unconscious state—the nightmare—the message of the mind is joined with the body, creating the reaction. To be clear, even though the events of the nightmare didn't actually happen, the body perceives it as real. Visualization is very similar, except that we are conscious and focused on a particular chosen outcome. When it comes to supporting health with visualization techniques, especially on a consistent basis, the mind is saturated with healing messages that can be passed along to the body.

Visualizing the steps toward our goals and the goals themselves can also give us a sense of control, confidence, and hope—powerful healing tools in and of themselves. When we have hope, we are more likely to take additional positive steps, consciously or not, that support a healing system.

I heard a story about a man who had endured serious damage to his arm due to an accident. He repeatedly visualized construction workers fixing the injuries in great detail. His doctors were shocked when they saw how quickly and perfectly his arm had healed. You might call it mind over matter.

When I was diagnosed in 2011, I remembered this story, and I decided to try it for myself before my brain surgery. I started to use the construction-worker scenario, but that didn't seem right for me. So I decided to use butterflies—but these were fierce butterflies, incredibly strong and powerful. I imagined those butterflies coming into my brain and taking pieces of the cancer away to the farthest reaches of the earth, dropping them off into the darkness from which nothing can return.

Sometimes the butterflies would be so powerful I could *hear* their wings and *feel* the wind as they were flying to get more and more of the cancer and take it out with force and intention. It was an army of intense, focused butterflies. I believed they were getting it out even before the surgery. The exercise calmed me, too. I felt I had a sense of control, but I also really believed my intention of removing it was working somehow.

Interestingly, although my neurosurgeon didn't know that I was visualizing butterflies, the day before the surgery, he told me to visualize him getting all of the cancer out, and then he said, "And I will do the same." His words rang like a bell, as I knew we were on the same page.

Since the official expectation was that the cancer would quickly come back worse than before—even with surgery, chemo, and radiation—I continued doing visualizations for many months to make sure that my brain, my mind, and my body were aligned to vanquish the cancer forever. After brain surgery, I took radiation and chemotherapy for five weeks and more chemotherapy treatment once a month for nine months after the radiation protocol. But honestly, even before the doctors told me I was stable—and that's the best you're going to get from the doctors when it comes to this kind of brain cancer—I *knew* I was free of cancer. Much earlier than that, my butterflies had started to get quiet; there was no more work to be done.

There are many ways to visualize something you want to have in your life. Here are a few steps to help you get started:

1. Sit in a comfortable position or lie down. Close your eyes. Take a couple of deep breaths and relax.
2. Think carefully about what you want and what your intentions are. The mental image of your goal should be very clear.

3. Take time to imagine a pleasing story in which you envision the specific steps, in detail, that lead to what you want—your goal. Then visualize the moment you achieve your goal.
4. Once you settle into the story you have created, believe in it and replay it over and over.

You might prefer to use a different or less-structured approach, which is fine. You are only limited by your imagination. Musicians develop automatic muscle memory by practicing the same piece of music many times over. Visualization, through the dance of the mind and the body, can do the same.

Massage

Some people consider massage a form of medicine, since it not only helps relax the body but also supports it in many other ways. Massage manipulates and relaxes soft tissue; increases the flow of blood and oxygen, which in turn increases energy levels; and decreases pain and stress. It can also help support the lymphatic system by filtering toxins from the bloodstream. Consistent use of massage can give your body and mind a powerful message of healing and well-being.

For example, if you are like so many who have trouble with too-tight shoulder muscles, regularly getting a massage will not only alleviate the tension (for a while at least) but also help create an awareness of what you might be doing to cause the tension. This can help to change or heal the root cause.

After you get a massage, it is important to drink a lot of clean water for a day or so, because the massage releases stored toxins within the body. Drinking plenty of water helps remove the toxins from your system. For the same reason, it's common for some people to feel sleepy afterward, wanting a nap or earlier bedtime than usual. You might even fall asleep during a massage. When this happens, your relaxed body is telling you what it needs—more sleep! When you feel tired, pay attention and give your body the extra rest it is yearning for.

If you were recently diagnosed with a serious illness, be sure to let your massage therapist know about it before setting the appointment. Sometimes therapists are not able to work with people until certain conditions have been met. In those cases, I would suggest reaching out to your doctor, who may have a good reference (like the local hospital) for massage services. It's always a good idea for those fighting illness to check with their doctor first when considering new activities like massage.

There are many benefits to getting a regular massage—for the body and the mind. Just lying down on a massage table can start the calming, stress-relief reaction. Plus, the gentle music and aromatic smell of oils we usually find there remind us that we are doing something good for us indeed.

Yoga

The first few times I tried yoga, I thought it was just about stretching, balancing, and feeling calm. But as time went on, I began to realize that yoga is about understanding the union of the physical, mental, and spiritual aspects of ourselves. It is a special space to be in.

From the gentle stretches, twisting, bending, and balancing of yoga, you work your muscles and spine, loosen your joints, stimulate circulation, and expand your lungs. Your mind can become quiet as it focuses on the poses and not the problems in your life. Your anxiety and stress levels will start to fall off, and you might even forget about them for a while. With the help of this process, you stretch your body, focus your mind, and flow to your spirit. It is very healing.

If you are new to yoga, I suggest that you start to learn yoga at a yoga studio so you can meet other students and take in the experience of the environment. Typically, teachers will speak very calmly and explain the stretches in a lightly dimmed room. They will encourage you to feel the positions properly, but you will not be pushed beyond your comfort level. The environment is meant to be supportive. Each time you complete a practice, you can expect to feel a sense of calm and wellness. It can be very powerful, because you are moving energy.

In addition to finding yoga classes at a yoga studio, many gyms and fitness centers offer yoga classes, or you can buy a yoga DVD to practice with at home. Yoga books that include pictures of the poses can be helpful, as well as yoga exercises and classes you can find for free online.

Acupuncture

Acupuncture is similar to qigong in that the goal is the same: to remove blocks so the qi—our life force—can flow freely. It is a key part of the Traditional Chinese Medicine (TCM) that I described earlier. When we get an acupuncture treatment, we typically lie down on a comfortable table in a quiet room, and the acupuncturist places tiny needles at key pressure points in the body. These points stimulate and release energy that is blocked, thereby opening the body's energy pathways.

Although the main goal of acupuncture is to allow energy to flow throughout the body, this ancient technique helps improve many health conditions. For example, some people experience relief from pain, pressure, sinus infections, tinnitus, joint injuries, menopause, menstrual cramp symptoms, and even side effects of chemotherapy. It is not typically a permanent solution but can offer relief for many people. Regardless, if it allows you to move your energy and unclog and open the body's energy pathways, it might be worth trying.

Music

Music can be a powerful way to heal and calm ourselves and to feel connected to other people. A particular lyric and melody can help us feel understood and help us understand ourselves, too. Listen to country music after a breakup, and you will understand how this works! Sometimes music is just about feeling good. And sometimes, that's exactly what we need.

Most of us have experienced hearing a special song that temporarily transports us to another time and space, a memory, an emotion. Maybe we remember it from a special event in our lives or the music we grew up with, or maybe it's just a new song we connect to. As a result of the music, we often feel compelled to move, dance, tap to the rhythm, hum, or sing the words. Whatever it is, this is the nature of music.

Music has been around for a very long time; in fact, it is said to predate language. It is believed that Neanderthals played music almost 40,000 years ago and that it evolved to help people communicate their emotions to more people, even allowing them to develop a group identity. We can see in our own lives how music can do this. Go to a concert of your favorite band, singer, orchestra, or candlelight mass at church on Christmas Eve, and you will experience the social bonding that music can offer.

But music can also be very singular and personal. When I got sick, I connected to a couple of songs that somehow became my elixir. They helped me through the surgery, the radiation, and the chemo. Every time I heard the music, I would get a huge smile on my face. It would calm me immediately, as if to say, "You are all right just as you are." So, I pulled out my old music and incorporated music as one of my healing tools. What an easy way to feel good.

Music can arouse the brain and create powerful emotional reactions. Natural "happy" hormones—like dopamine, a neurotransmitter supporting pleasure, and oxytocin, the "cuddle hormone"—are secreted by the brain, making us feel happy, calm, well, and understood. With just a few notes of a favorite song, we can access our brain's pleasure center. Consider the well-known initial notes of "Sweet Home Alabama" by Lynyrd Skynyrd or Elton John's "Tiny Dancer" or "The Four Seasons" of Antonio Vivaldi. Not only can music be pleasurable, natural, fun, and universal, it can also be healing.

Studies have shown that listening to calming music can reduce anxiety, lower heart and respiratory rates, reduce cardiac complications, lower blood pressure and heart rate, support the immune system, and reduce stress hormones during medical testing.[48] Furthermore, through music therapy, the clinical use of music intervention, researchers have found improved results for patients struggling with dementia, Parkinson's, stroke, and brain damage. Music therapy has also successfully helped to reduce asthma episodes, relieve pain, improve communication for those with autism, and improve sleep patterns.[49]

Music can stimulate the brain to awaken emotions, memory, and even physical abilities, which is especially helpful for those fighting illness, disease, or injury. It's easy to see why some consider music a form of medicine.

Raymond Bahr, MD, director of coronary care at St. Agnes Hospital in Baltimore, Maryland, said, "Without a doubt, music therapy ranks high on the list of modern-day management of critical care patients ... Its relaxing properties enable patients to get well faster by allowing them to accept their condition and treatment without excessive anxiety."[50]

So, whether you are fighting disease or not, don't forget to add a daily dose of your favorite music to lift your body and soul.

Joy

> *Mad Hatter: You're not the same as you were before; you were much more much-ier. You've lost your much-ness.*
>
> *Alice: My muchness?*
>
> *Mad Hatter: There. [Points to her heart] There's something missing.*[51]

Just like Alice in Lewis Carroll's *Alice in Wonderland*, sometimes we lose our *muchness* in the process of growing up and dealing with the pressures of life—and we know it. We just have no idea how to get it back.

Instead of feeling joy, many of us feel flat and overwhelmed. We spend a lot of time working and doing, but not *being*, not *living*. We tell ourselves it will be better when the big deal closes, when the kids graduate high school, when we get the new job, or when we retire. But the reality is, there is never a good time to ignore joy in your life. Never.

All we have is this very moment—not the future, not the past. If we don't take just a little for ourselves along the way, each day, we might not have the opportunity later because none of us can know when our expiration date will be. It would be handy if we could—but it is just not the nature of things here on planet Earth!

Beyond that sobering thought, the reality is that our lives can be richer and healthier if we allow ourselves some free, fun space to play in. Taking time for joy in our lives helps the mind expand perspective, relaxes the body, reduces inflammation, and supports the immune system. It also supports a spirit that wants to fly.

There are many things we can do to access joy if we are willing to make a conscious effort to find it. It is a path to the simple pleasures we are meant to feel and enjoy.

To start finding more joy, write a list of things you enjoy doing. I promise, it can be harder than you think. When I did this exercise the first time, I realized how entrenched I had been in my work and my kids. I was embarrassed that I couldn't easily remember simple, fun things I used to enjoy just for myself. Once you look, though, you discover that these things don't have to be big, expensive, or take an enormous amount of time to lift your spirits way up.

Allowing ourselves to let go of the worries of the day by taking a walk in the park or a hike in the woods, listening or playing inspiring music, reading a great book, creating something, or spending one-on-one time playing with a pet can help replenish our systems and certainly our mood.

As mentioned previously, Dr. Kelly Turner, in her book *Radical Remission*, researched over a thousand cases of unexpected remission from cancer. One of the cancer survivors she interviewed spoke about the power of watching comedians on a DVD at home to help her deal with her serious diagnosis.[52] She found that laughing and enjoying herself helped elevate her mood, gave her a needed break from her diagnosis, and made her feel joyful. When we laugh, especially when we laugh a lot, we produce those feel-good endorphins, which improve our health, not to mention our mind and spirit. Try feeling sad when you are smiling or laughing —you just can't do it.

As a side note, Saranne Rothberg survived her level 4 cancer diagnosis and created the ComedyCures Foundation (comedycures. org), which creates therapeutic, humorous entertainment for many types of people needing the medicine of laughter.

No matter what you choose to do to expand your joy, stick with it. Allow yourself to recognize that taking this time is important, even critical. When we do things to create more joy in our lives, we honor our commitment to loving ourselves. We begin to feel more alive and connected. Most of us would rather feel that way than having nothing left for ourselves except the weight of resentment.

Since we need joy, we shouldn't feel guilty about it, either. When we are on a plane and flight attendants give the flight instructions, they tell adults to put their oxygen masks on *first*, and only after that has been done should they help others. In the same way, taking time for joy is about doing something affirming for your health, your strength, and your ability to feel happy.

Once you choose what you want to do, carve out at least thirty minutes every day for something that gives you pleasure and joy. Then, once a week, try to give yourself up to two hours if you can. Treat this joyful time as a powerful and important time for you to be supported in all ways.

The riches from giving yourself this time can spill into the rest of your life as you begin tapping into your life energy. Finding time for joy reinforces self-love, healing, and balance. Your entire system will pay attention.

Write It Out

Writing is an effective tool with therapeutic benefits that helps us manage our thoughts and feelings through insight and connection. Struggling with life's challenges is part of the human condition, yet I believe we are meant to learn from these challenges and try to get to the other side of them somehow stronger, wiser, and better. Sometimes the best way to do that is to sit down, alone, with pen and paper, and share your most personal thoughts—the good, the bad, and the ugly.

Not only does writing help us create a record of our thoughts, documenting where we were in our lives when we sat down to write, but the process of unloading on paper can be very liberating and illuminating. Here are two journaling tools I believe are particularly effective.

Slash and Burn

I was taught this technique when I was diagnosed with cancer, and I found it a powerful way to release what was going on inside of me. Here's what to do:

Each day, for two minutes, write down your most private thoughts. Be painfully honest with yourself; after all, no one else is going to read it, just you. It doesn't have to be cogent or mean anything; it is just about expressing your deepest feelings even if they're not organized or even understandable. You could even just put down dashes of angry marks with words on top of them. You might be expressing yourself in anger, loss, sadness, frustration, or confusion—whatever you choose.

Be sure to time yourself with a timer. When the time is up, don't look at what you wrote. Instead, immediately shred it, burn it, or rip it up into tiny pieces. Whatever way you do it, it needs to go away. This technique can help you release your most base and true thoughts in a safe environment, so you can move out of the intense and often damaging energy you hold in your system.

Journaling Your Thoughts

To get started, buy a journal and keep it by your bed or in another secure spot, free from prying eyes. On a regular basis, write down your thoughts, feelings, fears, and hopes—anything at all. This process allows you to quietly and privately check in with yourself. The more you do this, the more you can learn about how you really feel—important information when it comes to lightening your emotional load. Sometimes you can even stumble upon *aha* moments, connections, pearls of wisdom, and self-understanding.

One of the nicest things about journaling is that you can reread past ideas, thoughts, and discoveries. With an updated lens, you can consider how you felt then and compare it to where you are now. It can be an opportunity to see how you grow and develop emotionally and even spiritually. I can attest to this, as I have had a journal since I was in the first grade. There is something about this process that keeps us honest, and I think that's particularly valuable.

Admittedly, some people will be drawn to this practice more than others, but even if you are not all that interested, I encourage you to try it anyway. You might be surprised at what comes out. Awareness is a powerful way to understand our truth.

Being in Nature

Have you ever walked out of your home or office and suddenly realized it is a beautiful day outside? The birds are chirping, the sun is shining, and, bathed in it, you feel good. With an extra skip in your step, you might even mention it to those we meet: "Great weather today!"

We know intuitively that being in nature helps us feel good. The renowned painter Claude Monet, who created the famous "Garden at Giverny" in France, said, "The riches I achieve come from Nature, the source of my inspiration." This is a sentiment shared by many painters drawn to nature.

Poets, too—such as John Keats, William Wordsworth, and Robert Frost—have found inspiration from nature in their art. If you haven't read the poem "I Wandered Lonely as a Cloud" by William Wordsworth since high school, you might just want to dust it off, as the poet expresses so beautifully the blissfulness of being in nature. This portion of the poem describes what he felt when he stumbled onto a patch of daffodils one day:

> I wandered lonely as a cloud
> That floats on high o'er vales and hills,
> When all at once I saw a crowd,
> A host, of golden daffodils;
> Beside the lake, beneath the trees,
> Fluttering and dancing in the breeze.

What is it then, that we see and feel in the artistry of painters, poets, and our direct connection to nature? I believe it is that we inherently understand that being in nature offers a unique energy we can tap into, which restores us.

Nature might just be the perfect expression of life, and being around it can be healing, calming, and invigorating. Before we lived in homes with air-conditioning, we lived more closely to the land and nature. Being in nature helps us reconnect to our roots, literally and figuratively.

When we spend time hiking in the woods, walking in parks filled with trees, wandering in botanical gardens, and even observing the flowers, birds, and trees around our homes or neighborhoods, our senses get ignited in a way nothing else can replicate. There is a pure honesty we can surround ourselves with when we are among nature. We *smell* the flowers, we *feel* the mist of the air and the sun on our faces, we *hear* the birds chirping, we *touch* the wet leaves of the bushes or the bark of a tree, and sometimes we *taste* wild strawberries and blackberries in the summertime.

As we enjoy our elevated senses through nature, it's not a surprise that our mind and body are similarly influenced by the process. Many studies have shown that spending time in nature can support our health and emotions. Benefits include reduced stress, lowered blood pressure and hormone levels, a calmer nervous system, improved immune system function, increased self-esteem, reduced anxiety, and fewer feelings of isolation. These, in turn, promote relaxation and an improved mood.[53]

Other studies have linked the benefits of being in nature to improved short-term memory, reduced inflammation, the elimination of mental fatigue, better vision, and a greater ability to focus. Outdoor time has also been associated with lower overall risk for early death, especially among patients with cancer, lung disease, and kidney disease.[54]

In addition, the sun naturally provides us with the necessary amount of vitamin D needed per day in just twenty minutes. Vitamin D is critical for maintaining a healthy immune system.

So long as the environment is a safe one, we can enjoy the physical and mental benefits of being in nature in just twenty to thirty minutes. A longer stint might offer extended benefits, but just being out there on a consistent basis can help us connect to Mother Nature.

For those who may not be as mobile as others or who live in cities with limited access to green spaces, there are other ways to access nature. Gardening, for example, and even caring for plants in your home can offer benefits from nature. When some of us find ourselves in hospitals, having plants and flowers around us in our room can significantly shorten our hospital stay; lessen the need for painkillers; lower the rate of pain, anxiety, and fatigue; and improve positive feelings.[55]

Still, there are even more creative ways we can access nature. One is to simply walk around on grass barefooted. It might sound a little strange, but the coolness and texture of the grass and the depth of the ground beneath our feet can help us rediscover the connection we have to the earth, which can help us feel more alive and well. This is sometimes called *grounding*. The idea is that the earth emits electrical charges that we can access when we connect to the earth directly. There have been studies about this technique that link it with healing attributes.[56]

For those fighting cancer or other illnesses, you might try my lawn-chair approach to accessing nature. When I was fighting cancer, sometimes I just didn't feel well enough to exercise or go on a walk (maybe some of you can relate), so instead, I would lie down outside in a lawn chair, surrounded by nature, the trees nearby and the sky above me, and I would take one of my naps there. Even in the winter, if the sun was out, I'd wrap myself up in warm clothes and blankets and rest there in support of my health and happiness. In this way, nature can come to us.

However you choose to access the natural world, I hope you will find your own brand of daffodils to inspire you on your journey.

Look deep into nature, and then you will understand
everything better.—Albert Einstein

Chapter 6

The Spirit: Going Deeper

I gasped to see the moonlight filling the room.
I could never have seen it but for the darkness.

The light needs the dark, and the dark needs the light. When we learn to make peace with all aspects of ourselves, including the light and the dark, we can begin a new journey with our spirit that enriches our ability to live fully, authentically, and healthfully.

The truth is, we are all fairly complicated, and each one of us walks through life in a different way for different reasons. Sometimes we don't understand our unique path, and we need help figuring it out. Going deeper into our souls can help us get the answers we seek, and although doing so is sometimes the hardest part of healing, it can be the most gratifying, too.

Support from the Inside Out

Sometimes we need the support of others to help us heal. Sometimes our hurts are not physical at first; they remain in our minds and thoughts as if they had just happened. Old hurts and outdated ideas need to be understood and moved out for good. Psychologists, psychiatrists, counselors, clergy, healers, and life coaches can help us unlock the old thoughts that bring us and our overall health down.

The benefits of this kind of work can be immeasurable. In my case, I discovered my coach/energy healer at my holistic doctor's office while I was in chemotherapy. I noticed a flyer for a Saturday seminar about sensitive people. Although I was certain I was not one of *them*, I was curious anyway and signed up for myself and one of my friends. It was a great class except for the part where I discovered, to my chagrin, that I *am* actually a sensitive person!

I started working with the energy healer and continued working with her for several years. My journey unfolded in this way, allowing me to learn many things about myself I didn't know—and things I needed, especially at that time. We covered a lot of ground: old stuff, new stuff, how to handle a brain cancer diagnosis, and those delicate-yet-critical areas we all fumble with. She used a variety of techniques as we worked together.

She used a technique that I had never heard of called *tapping*, or the Emotional Freedom Technique (EFT). It is a technique created from a combination of ancient Chinese acupuncture and modern-day psychology. The gentle process of tapping by using our hands to access the energy meridians—key energy points on the side of your hand, your face, and specific places on your chest and underarm—allows the patient to be guided and supported with a specific challenge that is creating stress or worry. I admit, it sounds kind of strange, but it can be surprisingly effective. Look for tapping videos on the internet, like those at www.thetappingsolution.com, to get a better idea of how it works.

What I discovered from this whole process was extraordinary support for my mind, body, and spirit. I was healing parts of myself, and my spirit was soaring again. I could never have handled my diagnosis and everything else that was going on without help. You don't have to be sick physically, either, to need support like this. It's good for anyone who needs a little help letting go of some of the heaviness we carry in our minds. A clearer mind can allow your spirit to flow naturally and can support the body as well.

I have encouraged many people to find emotional support to deal with illness, emotional upset, unbelievable stress, loss, and people just grasping for help generally. The vast majority of them, both women and men, have told me that doing so was "a game-changer" and "the only way I could have gotten through the worst crisis imaginable in my life."

Just like anything, it's important to find the right source of support for you based on your needs. If you feel comfortable, you can start asking other people for referrals. People who have been through similar things can be a good source, as well as local universities, your doctor, a local hospital, or a local church. Even holistic-oriented local magazines found at yoga studios, naturopaths, and health-food stores can be good sources. This is true especially if you are looking for holistic support like that provided by shamans, healers, and medical intuitives. The internet may also offer this kind of access as well.

Wherever you find therapists or support, be sure to interview them, at least on the phone. A short discussion about your general concerns and goals and their responses can tell you a great deal. You will want to know whether they have had experience working with people dealing with concerns like yours. You will also want to make sure you have a reasonably good rapport. The process requires *both sides* to want the creation of your desired goals. It's also important to know what the fee will be up front. Lastly, it's always a good idea to research their credentials and review the feedback from others, if possible.

When we find the right means of support, we have the opportunity to dump the heavy stuff in our emotional backpacks—the stuff we are tired of carrying, whether we know it or not. In this way, we give ourselves the chance to live more freely, with more happiness and understanding and more love for ourselves.

Letting Go—Perspective, Judgment, Forgiveness

Do I not destroy my enemy when I make them
my friend? —Abraham Lincoln

When we become aware of the power of perspective, our judgments, and the act of forgiveness, we empower ourselves by accessing our consciousness. By doing this, we find space for all kinds of healing.

Perspective

Perspective has to do with how we choose to see a given situation or event. Typically, our view of what we perceive is colored by our past, present, and future expectations. Perspective is always changing. *It is not finite.*

Someone asked me, "What was the most important thing you learned about fighting brain cancer and your other challenges during that time?"

I surprised myself by blurting out: "Perspective!"

No one was more surprised than me to discover the many gifts I would find as a result of fighting brain cancer. It took me some time to see how life can work in mysterious ways if we are open to it. My perspective at the beginning of my diagnosis was singular—"terrible"—but as the journey moved forward, I began to see my truth in a more inspired way. With this lens, for example, I was able to see that it was the discovery of the diagnoses (the darkness) that woke me up (the light) and allowed me to see the life changes I desperately needed to make in order to live fully and healthfully. And I am forever grateful for that.

Focusing on perspective allows us to be more fluid about old and new concepts in our lives. We learn to see that our ideas are not static. Our health can change. Our mindset can change. Physicists teach us that the walls and the floors around us are not as solid as we think. In fact, all things are made of space and atoms that vibrate with energy at its core. It is why buildings, objects, and even our bodies ultimately break down. They are not solid; they are the collective of energy and space. Things can change.

It can be an enormous relief when we realize this truth. We don't have to spend so much time being right! Maybe there are several ways to see the same situation or event. Maybe things are not always black and white. Grey is a good color too.

In my situation, I could have taken many different paths, not one right or wrong. By shifting my perspective, however, I began seeing opportunities to heal my mind, my spirit, *and* my body. The strange thing was, the more I opened my mind to what could be, the more came my way.

You can find a person who lives in a one-room clapboard house right by the railway tracks who wants for nothing—who is joyful and happy. You can also find people living miserably in multi-million-dollar homes, wanting more and more things to fill the empty feeling inside of themselves. It's about perspective.

How do you filter what you see every day? Does the perspective you choose help you or hurt you? Do you choose to have a grateful heart, or do you choose a heart that is never satisfied, always searching, hungry for more, and scared at its core?

Tools you can use to work with perspective include qigong, yoga, good sleep, exercise, meditation, prayer, writing, and finding emotional support. Just listing your blessings, even on a difficult day, can help balance a perspective gone awry.

Perspective goes hand in hand with judgment and forgiveness.

Judgment

Judgment deals with the everyday steps many of us take to dismantle others and ourselves by judging. Sometimes we act as if we are judge and jury about people and events in our lives. Some of us are particularly well-versed in this activity.

Being flexible with our perspective allows us to be less rigid in considering what might be possible and can help us reduce our natural tendency to judge others. When we judge other people, especially as a constant behavior, we carry a heavy negative energetic load in our own systems. Negativity begets negativity, and so on. You could say it hurts us as the judge more than it hurts the person being judged.

When we judge others, we judge ourselves. And we usually go after the parts of us we don't like too much or haven't dealt with at all. In this way, we are the mirror of our judgments. Like a boomerang, it comes right back to us.

Here's an example of how this can work. When I was in college at the University of Rochester in New York, I took many psychology classes, as it was one of my majors. In my senior year, when I was almost ready to graduate, I signed up for one of Professor Edward Deci's humanistic psychology classes.

The layout of the class was different from anything I had seen before at school. The chairs were organized in a circle so we could all see each other. The class was odd in many other ways, too, since the professor didn't lecture as I had been accustomed to. In fact, he often said nothing at all until someone had something to say. I assure you, that can be very unnerving.

For the first couple of classes, I didn't get it at all—until I had something to say. Professor Deci noticed my reaction to one of the other students, a woman who was older than everyone else in the class, maybe in her mid-thirties. In his unassuming way, he simply asked what was going on with me.

Although I was reluctant to share my thoughts at first, I did so in the spirit of the class. The gist of my numerous complaints was that, in my view, she was a bit annoying. She was something of a know-it-all, and she acted like she was better than the rest of us. I capped my grievances by explaining that every time she had something to say, it bothered me.

I thought I had made a very persuasive argument, and I was sure I would get support for my position from all involved. However, that didn't happen. No one said anything except the professor. All he said was, "What's it to you?"

Not prepared for this twist, I asked him what he was talking about. I thought it was obvious that the older student was the problem, not me. Again, he asked the question, "What's it to you?" At that moment, the balloon of my gleeful judgment popped, and I stood there naked, realizing it was about *me*, not her.

That day in class, I discovered how the older student was similar to another person I knew, someone I had unresolved issues with. I would ultimately understand that by putting the light on *my* inner conflict and healing it there, I could be free of it.

That being said, we are not perfect here on earth, and we will judge. The key, in my opinion, is to limit it as much as possible and understand it better when it does come up. Paying attention to the *pings*—reactions like the one I had to my classmate—offers an opportunity to understand what's really going on inside of ourselves. Once I saw the connection, the original feelings I had about the student changed.

The dynamic shifted to more of a curiosity about what I needed to learn through my reactions to her. I would learn through this process that when we are awake to our inner challenges, we have the opportunity to heal the broken parts of us.

A simple way to test your *judgment meter*—the rate at which you judge other people or even yourself—is to avoid judging anyone for an entire day. If you find yourself defaulting back into the world of judgment, consciously and intentionally pull your energy back. We are not judging today.

One of the main purposes of this exercise is to understand how much negative energy we waste by judging. Consistent awareness and working with releasing this energy can change the habit, allowing us to feel happier, lighter, and even healthier. And when we do judge, we have the opportunity to ask, "What's it to you?" You just might find out.

Forgiveness

> *The weak can never forgive. Forgiveness is the*
> *attribute of the strong.—Mahatma Gandhi*

Forgiveness is the act of letting go of judgments. The act of judgment burdens our systems. It helps to forgive, even if you do it just because it is better for *you* to do it. When we forgive others, and even ourselves, we give ourselves the chance to lighten our burdens and find more love in ourselves.

A lot has been written about letting go, and for most of us, it is much easier to say than do. On the heels of my diagnosis, another event—a business conflict—occurred that stunned and saddened me. I was furious and devastated. As the business matter went along, people told me to try to "let go" and "forgive." They told me that it would be healthier for me, especially since I was still fighting cancer. I knew that it was true, but I wasn't ready. Although I worked hard at it, it still took several years to get to forgiveness.

Ultimately, I came to the realization that it was not my job to carry the load of my judgment against another person. Although I couldn't understand it completely, I let it go to the highest levels of the spiritual realm—for me, that is God—knowing the ultimate judgment will be meted out there. *There,* all the information is in full view, where it should be. When I finally let it go, I was relieved and free, because it takes a lot of energy to hate another person.

For most of us, letting go and forgiveness take time. It is a process. Some days might be better than others. Ultimately, with the intention of slowly getting it out of our system, the pain, the hurt, and the shock can fade away and transform into something else—maybe even compassion for the other person.

I discovered three steps that helped me let go and get closer to the holy grail of forgiveness:

1. **Become aware that to let it go is self- loving.** When you let go, you free your mind from something old and musty and allow a new, healthier, more creative energy to come in. Ultimately, it has nothing to do with the other person who has affected you. It's about you, period.

2. **Invoke your will to release what you don't want anymore.** At some point, you may be ready to invoke your will to permanently release what is hurting you. You might realize it's just not worth holding on to it anymore. But it's still hard. When you stumble and get back into judgmental thinking, remind yourself how you are free when you let it go and recommit to forgiveness—for your sake. Set the goal of release, even if you are not there yet. Over time, you can get there.

3. **Use perspective to realize that situations and people are not absolute.** You can try to imagine the other person's perspective, although it might be hard to do, especially at the beginning. If the person was someone you knew, you might try to remember that individual's good qualities, appreciating the fact that you don't know all of the reasons why people do the things they do. None of us does. Remind yourself that it's not your job to obsess on the situation or try to psychoanalyze everything. Working with perspective can help loosen the grip of your view about the situation or person.

Although the process of forgiveness can be very healing, it doesn't necessarily mean we need to go back to the relationship that negatively affected us in the first place. In fact, many times the forgiveness acknowledges our self-love, and in our effort to maintain this sense of self, we are better served to let go of the judgment *and* the relationship completely.

It has been said that "there is no revenge so complete as forgiveness." It may take time to get there, but all of us have the ability to release the burden from ourselves by moving judgment to forgiveness and by working with perspective to get there. When we strive for this, we are closer to being in balance in a way that honors all aspects of ourselves—mind, body, and spirit.

Finding the Spirit

We don't need the name of the flower to understand its beauty.

The spiritual realm is one of three key aspects of balance and healing—the others being the mind and the body. Spirituality requires attention, awareness, consciousness, even effort. Unfortunately, at this time, there is a considerable amount of skepticism—or, worse, disinterest—about the spiritual realm. Some proudly scoff at spirituality and/or religion like it's a badge of honor (which is, of course, their right) and then retreat into their mind instead of their heart, where many truths live. I have to admit I have been there too.

But I have come to understand that spirituality is a critical—if not the most critical—aspect of our existence here on earth and beyond. I believe when we block this essence, our soul, we cannot be complete. It's part of each one of us. Why would we deny it—or at least, not be curious about it?

Just like physical exercise improves the body, spiritual exercise expands the soul. When we pray, meditate, practice qigong, use breathing techniques, or attend religious services that move us, for example, we give ourselves the chance to strengthen our spirit. In this way, we expand what can be possible for us. It's an opening to find truth, peace, and self-understanding.

In addition, conscious spiritual practice can have a positive effect on the body by improving the immune system and energy level, creating less anxiety and depression, and improving circulation, quality sleep, and breathing. These are just a few examples in which spirituality is good for our health.

I did not grow up with a formal religion of any kind, although I had some personal experiences I believed came from a higher realm. As a result, I had the sense that there was something bigger than just the things of this earth. I called it the *Universe* because the word *God* made me feel uncomfortable. This worked for most of my life—until I got sick.

During my healing process, I began to understand more about connections, energy, gifts from above, and coincidences that some might call supernatural. I felt an energy of unbelievable love and compassion. It might sound implausible, but there were people I had never met praying for me in prayer groups throughout the country— and I felt their support and love. Something was happening as a result of what seemed to be a pure nightmare. I began to feel God's love. I could not use the word *Universe* anymore, since it was no longer enough for what I was experiencing.

I began praying every day, and more than once if I needed it. In the beginning, I would get a feeling of safety and an extraordinary sense of love that I believed was God. Then I would receive some words, such as, *You've got this* or *You are loved.* I wondered where they came from. *Did I say that?* But over time, I knew exactly what it was: the love of God and angels.

As this journey unfolded, more extraordinary things, supernatural things, started to became commonplace in my world. Here's an example. I underwent radiation treatment every five days for five weeks. To keep me from moving during treatment, the nurse would hook the plastic mask I was wearing to the table I was lying on, creating a very strange and almost claustrophobic feeling. The following is what I wrote in my journal on the last day of my treatment:

Journal entry, August 19, 2011

At the very moment I finished my last radiation treatment, I was walking to the reception area to meet Jamie [my brother]. I had my head plastic thing, and I was showing it to him. He said to hold on because a news story on CNN would be coming right up. Literally at this very moment, as if on cue, this story starts with a woman named "Jennifer" who had a brain tumor ... Doctors didn't give her much hope, but, she said, "You can't live life with fear." She said, "Maybe I could live another 10 years or 25 years." As a result, she and her husband bravely decided to get pregnant anyway and against the doctor's advice. They were choosing to do something not based on fear.

Her message was to live your life anyway. It was exactly what I needed at exactly that moment. It was crystal clear to me. My brother, a true skeptic, and I felt that something extraordinary had just happened. That message—at that perfect time, with a name just like mine, with a diagnosis like mine—was telling me to stop worrying (which I was struggling with) and begin living a life worth living *no matter what.* I knew God was all over this message, and I was incredibly grateful.

Over time, the depth of my communication with other realms became even more mind-boggling—for me, at least. Remember, I didn't grow up with formal religion and hardly knew the lingo. But it didn't matter. I was becoming more deeply connected to this spiritual energy. I began to get messages, mostly at the twilight hours of bedtime, just as I was dozing off or later in the night, gently awakening me to "talk."

In the beginning, the visits were mostly to help me confirm that I was really accessing this realm, as you can imagine. Even though I was questioning what was happening, I was open and surrounded by love, and I was not afraid. As these visits continued, my understanding of love and wisdom, the nature of men and women, and the nature of my spirit grew, and I was becoming whole. I was being taught a high-level understanding of deep truths of our experiences here on earth and beyond it.

Because these conversations were so incredible, I started writing them down. I felt like a scribe in the middle of the night as I tried not to awaken my sleeping husband. One of the first ones was as simple as this: "The place of love is right here. Nothing else needs to be done. It is all here. It has always been here. It is here for you now. There is grace and love and truth here."

As my connection with the spiritual realm grew even deeper, the level of discussion became more intense, too, with conversations often lasting more than an hour. People in my family who had passed away also came in and would share wisdom and their history on earth. These were things I could never have known. They would often give me some kind of confirmation, a nugget I could use with my family here on earth to help confirm the messages were real.

In this master class, as it was explained to me, I learned that love is the most powerful energy, and it is infinite. I learned that I was loved in this way, and all souls are loved in this way. We are all very special. I was taught how to go to my mountain, in my mind's eye, when the things of earth were getting too sticky or heavy. We are not meant to live that way all the time. I was shown how to elevate myself spiritually, to breathe again, and to find a fresh perspective until I was ready to come down to earth again, although a little lighter than before.

We talked about other things, too, like decisions I had made, and my truth and purpose here on earth. I also learned that we are all connected. We are all sisters and brothers. They showed me that although this is true, most of us here on earth allow ourselves to believe we are not. And there is a culture that tries to sell or access power by focusing on distinctions instead of wholeness. We are more like each other than anything else! Are some of us elephants and others trees? That's ridiculous. At the core, we are the same.

More than that, I learned that everything is connected. Even our words and thoughts have an impact on all things. It's as if what we say, think about, and do have a reverberation, like a rock thrown in a lake creating ripples. I was told to be careful about the words I use since they matter. A daunting thought, especially since many of us are so casual about the things we think about and say.

Masaru Emoto, author of the *New York Times* bestseller *The Hidden Message in Water*, tested this concept. His premise was based on the fact that we humans are mostly made of water (70 percent) and that water has the ability to memorize information. He set out to prove it with physical evidence by taking various types of water in petri dishes until the frozen water created crystals. Then he would photograph the crystal images. Certain kinds of water, such as tap water with chlorine, did not form any crystal designs, but natural water created complex crystal patterns—each one different, like snowflakes.

He then expanded his research in photographing ice crystals by observing the effects of music on water. Classical music created well-formed crystals with unique characteristics. Heavy metal music resulted in malformed crystals. When he further applied this technique to certain words (written and taped facing the water) and statements (spoken to the water), the results were stunning. In his research, kind, loving words and thoughts created beautiful images in the water, while the opposite—hateful thoughts and words—created ugly and almost scary images in the water.

If we consider the water to be a symbol of our spirit, a conduit of energy, we can see how powerful our thoughts and words can be. Through the unusual research of Masaru Emoto, we can understand that both sides of the coin—loving words and thoughts and hurtful ones—have an impact, just like the reaction from the rock thrown in the lake. Maybe the biggest decision comes from your free will in choosing what you want to put out there for yourself and others.

Being aware and choosing higher-level energy in our thoughts and words can elevate the spirit. Yet the opposite is also true. Choosing low-level thoughts, like hate, can pull us away from lightness, freedom, and truth, and feed fear instead. But even when we choose lightness and high-minded thoughts, the goal isn't to be perfect, because we are not. It's more of a commitment to try to be a little better every day than we were the day before. And when we falter—and we will— we pull ourselves back up and try yet again to be the best version of ourselves we can be. And that is all we can ask of ourselves.

With conscious thinking and living as a foundation, we can individually make powerful positive changes in our lives and the lives of others if we choose to. Similarly, the collective of all people can create a better world if we choose to. It has happened.

Consider some of the massive tragedies that have occurred in recent years—9/11 in New York City, the Pentagon, and Flight 93; children attacked in 2012 at Sandy Hook Elementary in Connecticut; and the 2011 tsunami in Japan, just to name a few. In these situations, people's hearts united with pure compassion, love, and connection with others they didn't even know.

There was an understanding, a unique fundamental closeness. The collective was awake for a while. When we consider the fact that this energy exists, it helps to understand the powerful and important role we play individually, and the role of our spirit, our essence. But it begs the question: Can we stay awake without needing tragedy to wake us up?

Eckhart Tolle, author of *The Power of Now*, a must-read *New York*

Times bestseller, writes about the power of the very moment in which we live. He explains we do not have a past or a future and that there is only this moment—the Now. Then, it will be gone, and you will have a new moment, and on and on. It is constant creation. This very moment is inspired. He says that whether you call it *God* or *presence*, it is our core essence. When we are conscious, we can access this moment. When we are unconscious, we are not fully here, and we miss an important aspect of our spirituality.[57]

I began to understand that my spiritual experiences were happening because I had let God into my life. That first night at the hospital, on the day of my diagnosis, when I prayed to God, I surrendered myself to what had always been there. I had been blocking it because the limits of my mind wouldn't let me find the connection. But when I dropped my facade, my ego—the crafted layers I had created for myself—I was exposed to who I really was— the unadorned, pure aspects of me. And God was there.

In *The Power of Now*, Tolle explains the phenomenon this way: "As far as the still unconscious majority of the population is concerned, only a critical limit-situation has the potential to crack the hard shell of the ego and force them into surrender and so into the awakened state." He explains a limit-situation happens "through some disaster, drastic upheaval, deep loss, or suffering your whole world is shattered and doesn't make sense anymore." He continues to explain that situations like this don't always do it, but the "potential is always there."[58]

Further, he says: "Limit-situations have produced many miracles" as those involved were "forced into surrender. In this way, they were able to enter the state of grace with which comes redemption: complete release from the past."[59]

Traumatic situations can be like tripwires that open the mind to this realm. If we nurture it, our spirit can grow and become richer and deeper. In my case, by being open to the spiritual realm, focusing on it, and exploring it, I became stronger, clearer, and more balanced. I was changing. *I was awake.* As a result of my spiritual awakening,

I began to research people with similar experiences. I found a lot of information regarding people who had life-and-death experiences.

Another bestselling book that captivated me was the story of orthopedic surgeon Mary C. Neal, MD, in her book *To Heaven and Back: A Doctor's Extraordinary Account of Her Death, Heaven, Angels, and Life Again.* Dr. Neal was on a kayaking trip in South America when her kayak was submerged in the water for a long period of time. Pinned down, she began to cross over to heaven. After a significant period of time, her group found her "purple, bloated, oxygen-starved body." They dragged her to shore, and ultimately, miraculously, she came back to life.

Her injuries were intense, requiring several operations and surgeries and more than a month in the hospital. Through her experience, she explains in great detail, and with great candor, the nature of heaven, the nature of God and angels, our purpose on earth, and the nature of the spiritual journey overall.

She shares the following passage to explain part of what she learned from her journey:

> I knew that I had been given the many experiences of
> my life, my death, and my return so that I could use
> my experiences and observations to help others stop
> doubting and just believe—believe that spiritual life
> is more important than our physical one. Believe that
> God is present and at work in our lives and our world.
> Believe that we are each a beautiful part of an intricate
> tapestry of creation. Believe there is no such thing as
> "coincidences."[60]

Here, she describes how her life has permanently been transformed as a result of her journey to the other side:

> This knowledge has changed the way I interact with
> my medical patients. I recognize how significantly a
> patient's emotional and spiritual health impacts their

recovery, and I am able to use my own experiences to give them hope, even in the midst of substantial disability or injury. I often pray for my patients and, occasionally, with them. I now see my professional role as more of a "healer" rather than of someone who just "fixes" their mechanical problems.[61]

Amen!

Another book that is helpful in understanding the nature of spirituality is *The Untethered Soul* by Michael A. Singer. Here, he discusses the nature of God:

> Your relationship with God is the same as your relationship with the sun. If you hide from the sun for years and then choose to come out of your darkness, the sun would still be shining as if you had never left. You don't have to apologize. You just pick your head up and look at the sun.
>
> It's the same way when you decide to turn toward God—you just do it. If, instead, you allow guilt and shame to interfere, that's just your ego blocking the Divine Force. You can't offend the Divine One: Its very nature is light, love, compassion, protection, and giving. You can't make it stop loving you. It's just like the sun. You can't make the sun stop shining on you; you can only choose not to look at it. The moment you look, you'll see it's there.[62]

The story of Anita Moorjani is an extremely compelling one. In her book *Dying to Be Me: My Journey from Cancer, to Near Death, to True Healing*, Moorjani tells the story of being ravaged by cancer, falling into a coma, and living her last days on earth. She recounts her incredible experience of leaving her body, hearing the doctors in the hallway talking about her case, entering heaven, and, ultimately, coming back to earth. And if that's not interesting enough, her cancer *completely went away* nearly five weeks after she awakened from her coma.

In her travels to the other side, she realized many things she could not otherwise understand here on earth. One of them was that "God isn't a being, but a state of being … and I was now that state of being."[63]

She further explains: "There I was, without my body or any of my physical traits, yet my pure essence continued to exist, and it was not a reduced element of my whole self. In fact, it felt far greater and more intense and expansive than my physical being—magnificent, in fact."[64] In this new realm, she discovers with great clarity the causes of her illness and ultimate coma. The path she had been following for many years was hurting her. She says: "Just look at my life path. Why, oh why, have I always been so harsh with myself? Why was I always beating myself up? Why was I always forsaking myself? Why did I never stand up for myself and show the world the beauty of my own soul?"[65]

Being flooded with unconditional love and acceptance, she writes: "I was able to look at myself with fresh eyes, and I saw that I was a beautiful being of the Universe. I understood that just the fact that I existed made me worthy of this tender regard rather than judgment. I didn't need to do anything specific; I deserved to be loved simply because I existed, nothing more and nothing less."[66]

Once she was able to see her truth in this expansive, loving way, she chose to come back to earth. Her newfound awareness allowed her to discard her old ideas for new ones, and that allowed her body to begin healing at a rapid rate. Her awakening and consciousness of the connections of all things and her newfound deep sense of self-love helped her to heal her body in a miraculous way.

Although these stories seem extraordinary, and they are, that doesn't mean you can't access this realm and create your own extraordinary understanding. It's possible for you too. I have come to recognize that the energy from this higher realm exists close to all of us, but there is so much noise and so many distracting *things* in our world that we are easily pulled away from it.

Without conscious awareness, we don't allow ourselves to be silent, to quiet our minds, to focus and connect to our souls. In this way, we block ourselves from accessing this very real dimension. As discussed earlier, the things of earth are temporary, while the spirit is infinite.

There are many people who connect to the other side and get messages, receive signs, and see or feel angels and even God. They don't even have to get sick or shocked to access it—they just can. The truth is, we all have this ability if we open ourselves to it.

There are also people who believe in God, the Universe, but have never experienced a personal moment or a real connection to it. I believe messages, connections, and miracles from the other realm come to us all the time. However, many of us are such skeptics, we question the feeling and often reject it, thereby missing the opportunity to access this loving energy.

As a result, many of us haven't expressed this part of ourselves, maybe ever, and our connection to it is weak. But by continually exploring your soul, you can deepen your relationship to it and experience a deep sense of peace and understanding. I don't believe we can completely heal or live fully without being connected with the spirit in some way.

There are many tools in this book—such as breathing techniques, qigong, yoga, meditation, music, joy, and prayer—that can awaken a spiritual moment without even trying. It will just be there. And since everything is connected, we can find our spirit virtually anywhere.

Just walking around in nature and paying attention to what you see can be a spiritual experience if you are open, almost childlike, and fluid about these possibilities. Being out in nature can be a perfect time to remember that God is like a beautiful flower: we don't have to understand Him completely to know His beauty. And so go the gifts of the spiritual realm. Some people find a connection to this realm by reading ancient texts like the Bible or attending worship services. Being surrounded by people focused on the same goal can be powerful medicine.

Regardless of what you choose to do, choose something that can help connect you to this important aspect of your deepest self. Just being open is a great place to start.

Chapter 7

Putting It All Together

I was thrilled to see the 2018 Nobel Peace Prize in Medicine awarded to two cancer immunotherapy researchers. I was jumping for joy—literally. James Allison of the United States and Tasuku Hanjo of Japan discovered a way to *unblock* a sneaky cancer process that otherwise *blocks* the immune system from fighting a particular type of brain cancer.

The big story for me wasn't the impressive back door they found; it was the acknowledgment that the immune system is a powerful and fundamental healing agent. The immune system fights to keep us healthy and fights extra hard when we are not. Our bodies are built for this.

As I discussed earlier in the book, if we can get sick, why can't the opposite also be true? We can heal, and we have an important role to play in healing ourselves. I probably wouldn't be here if I hadn't believed and acted on this premise. It's also curious that, although we know our bodies are built to heal, when we become seriously ill, many of us forget this truth and turn exclusively to surgery and drugs for help.

When we flood our body, mind, and spirit with healing tools like the ones in this book, we can directly affect many aspects of ourselves, including the immune system. And when we support the immune system, we give ourselves a fighting chance to beat and remove illness, bacteria, infection, cancer, and other miscreants hanging around in the body. Even better, if we maintain a strong immune system, we can prevent many of these diseases from taking hold in the first place. The immune system is like our personal Special Ops unit—collective warriors fighting for us 24/7.

But we have to take care of our immune system to be co-warriors in this fight. When we don't give ourselves plenty of sleep, or eat nutritious foods, or exercise, among other things, we knock our immune system down, making it easier for illness to creep in and stay. Similarly, when we manage our nervous system and minimize stress, we can live a more balanced and joyful life in addition to a healthy one by limiting inflammation in the body. Using the tools in this book—such as meditation, breathing techniques, prayer, and unloading judgment—we can support the three pillars.

It's all connected, and it's not really complicated. When we choose to support ourselves with intention, care, self-love, and action, we do better, and we feel better.

In *The Case for Hope*, I have shared many simple and powerful tools that can support the mind, the body, and the spirit. I have offered my story as a backdrop from which I hope a more universal truth can be gleaned. I have described the nature of the world we live in, as unsteady as it is; the stress we experience in daily life; the limitations of many traditional doctors; the power of change; and the imperative of engaging the will to make healthy changes.

We learned about the body as a critical foundation for those interested in healing and those just interested in living a healthier, happier life. We discussed many simple methods that support us in important ways, including breathing techniques, exercise, drinking clean water, proper sleep, *real* nutrition, and dealing with toxins.

We discussed the mind and discovered how powerful we really are and how mindfulness can directly affect physical change in our bodies and our lives. To this end, we discussed the beautiful tools of qigong, yoga, music, joy, writing, prayer, meditation, visualization, acupuncture, massage, and being in nature.

We discussed the hidden gem—the Spirit, the space we do not touch or see but understand is part of us anyway. As we journeyed into the aspects of the Spirit, we started with the basic but brave steps of getting professional care to lighten the load we carry. We talked about the importance of perspective, the heaviness of judgment, and the release of forgiveness. Then we delved into the essence of ourselves, our souls, and discovered we are all very much loved and connected to one another. We learned that being open to another realm can offer an incredibly rich and healing path to the deepest parts of our selves.

I learned these tools one by one and grew to understand that the aggregate of all of these things was healing me. Now the information is laid out for those who come after me. I don't want it to feel like an overwhelming firehose of information. That's the last thing you need.

For that reason, I encourage you to start by identifying a few things that seem to jump out at you as an area of need or curiosity. You might choose to add more tools every couple of weeks or so until you have created your own personalized tool kit for health, balance, and joy. The concepts and tools in this book are intended to be a loving gift, guiding you to make changes in your life so you can "live a life worth living," no matter what.

Conclusion

Our "walk" in life is an imperfect journey. We are built to make mistakes, lose, win, and experience grace and hardship. It is the nature of things here. How we choose to manage these experiences defines our spiritual growth and the quality of our mind and body.

The tools discussed here are like bridges—portals of transportation and transformation. Whether it is music, meditation, exercise, good sleep, joyfulness, or spiritual practice, these bridges can alter our sense of consciousness and make us better, more whole, and more ourselves.

There are all kinds of bridges in life. Thinking about what you'd like to see on the other side can help you take the steps needed to get there. The process requires that you pay attention and stay engaged. No one else can do that but you, because the path comes from the core of yourself, your deepest wants and needs.

Hope is the spark from which change can come. As we evolve, we create. In so doing, we can generate health and happiness by letting go of old dynamics and replacing them with new ones, so that, as mentioned previously, the caterpillar can be transformed into a butterfly.

Do you know where you want to go? Do you know what your destination might look like? Are you willing to take the steps you need to get there? I encourage you to follow your unique, inspired path. There is no right or wrong. No one is like you. You are special. Love deeply, as love is the path, the way, the light, and the case for hope.

Appendix A

A Beginner's Guide to Healthy Foods

PROTEIN SOURCES

Poultry

Organic chicken and turkey

Fish

Consume wild-caught seafood when possible. Best choices are:

cod	flounder
trout	sardines
wild salmon	herring
tilapia	mackerel
haddock	

Note:

Consumption of large fish such as tuna, shark, swordfish, and marlin should be limited, since they can contain more mercury than the smaller fish listed above. Too much mercury can be harmful to one's health.

Pork/Beef

Choose local, unprocessed meats like pork and beef.

Note:

Generally, it's a good idea to limit pork and beef intake. They are hard for the body to digest, and that can result in inflammation in the body.

Dairy

cottage cheese   eggs: organic or free range, if possible
Greek yogurt—without sugar   kefir
Add natural fruits and a touch of local honey, for added taste.

Note:

Kefir is a cultured, fermented milk with antibiotic and antifungal properties and helps to support gut flora.

Other Protein Sources

almonds/almond butter	chia seeds	peas
amaranth	chickpeas	pumpkin seeds
black beans	hemp seeds	quinoa
broccoli	lentils	spinach
brown rice	oatmeal	sweet potato
Brussels sprouts	peanut butter (organic)	tahini
		tempeh

Note:

Try to eat natural protein whenever possible. Avoid processed protein drinks, which are usually filled with sugar and other processed ingredients; lack natural nutrients and fiber; and can create inflammation.

OTHER GOOD FOOD SOURCES

Legumes (Beans)

adzuki	fava	lentil
black	garbanzo/chickpea	lima
black-eyed peas	Great Northern	navy/red
cannellini	kidney	pinto

Note:

You can buy dried beans and soak them or choose BPA-free canned beans that are ready to be consumed. BPA (bisphenol A) is a synthetic estrogen found in the epoxy coating of food cans that is linked to various health problems. Search for canned beans that identify "BPA-free" on the label.

Nuts and Seeds

almond butter	coconut	pumpkin seeds
almonds	flaxseed	sesame seeds
Brazil nuts	hazelnuts	sunflower seeds
cashews	peanuts (organic)	walnuts
chia seeds	peanut butter (organic/no sugar added)	

Note:

- You might make a trail mix of your favorite nuts, seeds, and raisins and place into a container for healthy, easy-access snacks during the day.
- Choose jars of nut butters where oil rises to the top. Avoid commercial brands containing hydrogenated oils and sugar.
- Eat nuts and seeds raw when possible.

Vegetables

artichoke	green beans
asparagus	green/red/yellow pepper
beets	kale
butternut squash	lettuce, green and romaine
broccoli	mushrooms
Brussels sprouts	onions
cabbage (also fermented)	peas
carrots	spinach
cauliflower	sweet potatoes
celery	tomatoes
collards	turnip greens
eggplant	yams
fennel	yellow squash
garlic	zucchini

Note:

- Eat plenty of vegetables with a variety of colors and types each day.
- Limit starchy vegetables, such as potatoes, yams, corn, and peas.
- See Appendix B: When to Choose Organic.

Fruit

apples	grapefruit	peaches
avocado	honeydew	pear
banana	kiwi	pineapple
blackberries	lemons	plums
blueberries	lime	pomegranate
cantaloupe	mango	raspberry

cranberries	nectarine	strawberry
cherries	oranges	tomatoes
coconut	papaya	watermelon
grapes		

Note:

- Enjoy a variety of colors and types each day but try not to eat more fruit than vegetables and other healthy foods.
- See Appendix B: When to Choose Organic.

Dairy

In addition to the dairy items listed in the protein list above, butter (organic if possible; not margarine) and ghee (clarified butter) are healthy choices.

Note:

- Butter is a saturated fat, and our bodies can process it. Margarine, however, is a trans fat, which can be harmful to the arteries and can negatively affect hormone balance.
- Ghee is clarified butter made by gently heating and filtering cow's milk butter. It has antioxidant benefits, among others.

Beverages

clean water: add squeezed fruit, lemon, or frozen fruit if desired.
organic herbal teas
green tea

Healthy Fats

avocado	extra virgin olive oil	ghee
coconut oil	fish oil	

Whole Grain, Ancient Grains, and Grain Products

amaranth	kamut
barley	millet
brown rice	oats (organic)
buckwheat	quinoa
bulgur (cracked wheat)	sorghum
chia	spelt
farro	teff
flaxseed	whole wheat
freekeh	wild rice

Note:

- **Whole grains**—The term *whole grain* describes grains that include the bran, endosperm, and germ, comprising a complete grain. *Refined* or *enriched* grains, such as white rice and white bread, are highly processed and have most or all of the nutrients and fiber removed. This leaves only the starch (endosperm), which can cause blood-sugar-level spikes and inflammation in the body. *Whole wheat, whole grain wheat, 100 percent whole wheat,* and *cracked wheat* are examples of whole grains we should choose.

   When you visit the grocery store, beware of the slick marketing that may suggest a product is *whole grain* or *whole wheat* when it's not. For example, *wheat* is not the same or as good as *whole wheat,* and ingredients will sometimes include whole wheat as well as the processed grains we seek to avoid, such as enriched grains.

   Your best defense is to read the ingredients for yourself. These healthier choices can be found in bread, cereal, crackers, and pasta. In addition to whole wheat, brown rice (also a whole grain) can be a good choice.

- **Ancient grains**—Ancient grains and ancient wheat are kinds of grains that have been around for thousands of years. They are simpler grains and less compromised than the highly processed wheat we typically see at the grocery store. Examples of these ancient grains include barley, bulgur, farro (including spelt, emmer, and einkorn), freekeh, kamut, millet, oats, sorghum, and teff.
- **Grain products or pseudo-cereal grains.** These are ancient foods that are not actually grains, but they are grown and cooked the same way. In fact, they are seeds. Examples include amaranth, buckwheat, chia, flaxseed, quinoa, and wild rice.

Herbs and Spices

basil	cloves	parsley
black pepper	coriander	rosemary
cardamom	cumin	saffron
cayenne pepper	curry	sage
caraway	garlic	St. John's Wort
celery seed	ginger	thyme
cilantro	mustard	turmeric
cinnamon	oregano	

Natural Sweeteners

apricots	prunes
dates	pure maple syrup
figs	raisins
fresh fruit	raw honey (local if possible)
	stevia

Note:

Limit intake of natural sweeteners

Healthy Snacks

fruit	nuts and seeds
trail mix	nut bars—with good ingredients

hummus or almond butter with carrots and celery stalks

Note:

- It's a good idea to keep healthy snacks around so you avoid getting so hungry you'll eat anything. You're going to get hungry, so prepare for it!
- Be sure to carefully review the ingredients of nut bars before purchase. Many homemade healthy versions can be found online.

Dessert Ideas

Dark chocolate: Dark chocolate is lower in sugar than milk chocolate and doesn't spike blood sugar levels due to its high fat content.

Fresh fruit: Add yogurt and a small amount of raw honey to berries and any other fruit.

Frozen fruit: sorbet, with no added sugar or fructose.

Popsicles: blended fruits frozen into popsicles.

Frozen yogurt fruit: With a dessert maker such as Yonanas, use frozen fruit to mimic frozen yogurt. Surprisingly delicious.

Frozen bars: Homemade frozen bars can be made with almost anything! Try almond butter, organic peanut butter, cocoa, maple syrup, coconut oil, and/or puffed quinoa. Chill in freezer.

Green Drinks: Some Common Ingredients

Greens	Veggies	Fruit	Seeds/Nuts
collards	beets	apples	almonds
kale	broccoli	avocado	chia
romaine lettuce	cabbage	bananas	coconut meat
spinach	carrots	berries	flax seed
Swiss chard	celery	lemon	hemp
	cucumber	mango	sesame
	pepper (green, red)	orange	walnuts
		pineapple	
		strawberry	

Herbs/Spices	Other
basil (fresh)	coconut oil
chili powder	keifer
cinnamon	nut milk, such as almond milk
ginger	protein powder—free of sugar
nutmeg	water (clean)
pink Himalayan salt	yogurt (plain)
turmeric	

Note:

- To make green drinks, blend together vegetables, fruits, herbs, spices, nuts, and water or almond milk to create a delicious healthy drink filled with nutrients your body and mind will love. There are a few high-end blenders that are powerful enough to make these beverages. Blendtec and Vitamix are popular brands. However, I have seen some more traditional, and less expensive, blenders do a reasonably good job too if they include a "smoothie" choice.
- As you create your masterpieces, try to have more veggies than fruit. Aim for a 3-to-1 ratio to maximize the health benefits.

Appendix B

When to Choose Organic

Buy Organic

apples
blueberries
celery
cherries
coffee
corn
cucumbers
dairy
grapes
green collards
hot peppers
kale
leafy greens
meat
nectarines

oats
peaches
pears
potatoes
snap peas
soy
spinach
strawberries
sweet bell peppers
tomatoes
wheat
wine
yellow summer squash
zucchini

Organic Isn't Necessary

asparagus
avocado
banana
broccoli
cabbage
cantaloupe
cauliflower
corn on the cob
eggplant

grapefruit
kiwi fruit
mango
mushrooms
onions
pineapple
sweet peas
sweet potatoes
watermelon

Appendix C

Food Additives to Avoid

Acesulfame-K (Sunett and Sweet One)	Artificial sweetener that is two times sweeter than sugar. Cancer-causing in studies on rats.
Aspartame (Nutrasweet and Equal)	A sweetener sometimes associated with headaches, nausea, memory loss, seizures, vision loss, even cancer. Can increase desire for more sweeteners. May be found in diet sodas, sugar-free foods, and candies.
Butylated hydroxy anisole and Butylated hydroxytoluene (BHA and BHT)	Chemicals typically found in certain foods, such as potato chips and vegetable oils. They are potentially harmful to the liver and kidneys, and a suspected carcinogen. They can cause allergic reactions as well as neurological problems. (Kids can feel hyper.)
Evaporated cane juice	A raw sugar made from sugarcane juice with scant trace minerals. Beyond that, it's no better than regular sugar. You will find it in breakfast cereals, cheese crackers, "healthy" labeled cereal bars, soups, and sauces.

Food Colorings: **Blue 1 and 2, Red 3, Red 40,** **Green 3, Yellow 6**	Dyes that create health problems from cancer to thyroid problems in animal studies. Some studies have found links to serious behavioral problems in children.
High-fructose corn syrup	Inexpensive and highly processed additive associated with obesity. It spikes blood-sugar levels, has limited nutritional value, and is mostly made of GMO (genetically modified organism) corn in the US. Found in almost everything, including ketchup, cakes, crackers, and drinks.
Hydrogenated or partially hydrogenated vegetable oils	Fats, also known as trans fats, that create free radicals. A type of saturated fat that raises bad cholesterol, which can lead to heart disease and lowers good cholesterol, which helps the formation of cell membranes and hormones. Found in frozen meals, baked goods, cookies, crackers, and doughnuts. Look for labels that say *no trans fats* to avoid getting any.

Monosodium glutamate (MSG)	Flavor enhancer creating negative reactions in some people, such as headaches, nausea, and allergic reactions. Sometimes found in Chinese restaurant food and soups. In the US, it is frequently hidden as an ingredient under names like *natural flavor* and *autolyzed yeast extract*.
Olestra	A synthetic fat that stops fat from being absorbed by the body and also prevents essential vitamins from being absorbed. Primarily found in potato chips. Some people report symptoms like vomiting and diarrhea from use.
Potassium bromate	This chemical is a known carcinogen found in breads, pizza dough, and fast-food burger buns. Look for bromate-free processed foods.
Propyl gallate	Keeps fats and oils from going rancid. A suspected carcinogen. Found in processed meats, chicken stock/broth, chewing gum.

Sodium chloride	Common table salt stripped of beneficial minerals and trace elements. It also often contains aluminum (a toxic metal) as a drying agent. This refined salt is found in most prepared foods, including cheese, pickles, and soy sauce. Choose pink Himalayan salt instead.
Sodium nitrite or nitrate	A preservative and taste/color enhancer in meats and lunch meat. It is a potential carcinogenic nitrosamine and a potential cause of forms of cancer.
Sulfites	Potassium sulfite and sodium bisulfite aim to improve the color of foods, such as dried fruit, dehydrated soup or noodle mixes, syrups, pickles, shrimp, cookies, crackers, and beet sugar. Sulfites are also found in red wine and beer. Some people experience acute asthma attacks, headaches, cough, and skin rash due to sulfites.

67

Other Offenders and Potential Offenders

GMOs (Genetically Modified Organisms)

GMOs are man-made crops and animals that could not grow naturally. The topic is very controversial. Although we have been breeding animals, fruits, and vegetables for a long time, we breed within the same species, merging two different types of dogs to create the nonallergenic goldendoodle, for example. In the case of GMOs, the biotech companies splice the genes from one species (for example, a gene from a bacterium that can resist certain chemicals) into a completely different species (for example, a soybean seed), creating a Frankenstein-ish result in our food.

The largest company creating genetically modified foods, Monsanto (now named Bayer due to a merger), has been in the chemical business for over a hundred years, selling pesticides, herbicides, and fungicides. You might recognize some of their brand chemical names: DDT, PCBs, agent orange, and Roundup, an herbicide that contains glyphosate. This is why people are very nervous that the chemical companies are now in the food business.

Concerns with this process include the amount of the chemicals in and on our food, the chemical water runoff, and the unanswered questions about the safety of these lab-created products. Several countries have banned GMOs, but not the United States. Furthermore, there are no requirements in the United States to disclose GMOs in our food. If you are concerned about GMOs, choose products with labels like Non-GMO Project Verified or Certified Organic.

The Non-GMO Project, a nonprofit organization that offers third-party verification and labeling for non-GMO food and products, lists the following crops in commercial production as high-risk: alfalfa, canola (90 percent of the US crop), corn (93 percent of the US crop), papaya, soy (94 percent of the US crop), sugar beets (99 percent of the US crop), and zucchini and yellow squash.[68]

Maltodextrin

Maltodextrin is made of corn, rice, potato starch, and sometimes wheat. The process results in a white powder. Maltodextrin suppresses good bacteria in the gut, and its glycemic index is higher than table sugar.

Mono-Diglyceride Carrageenan and Guar Gum

We don't need either of them. They're possibly carcinogenic (in large amounts) and may also create inflammation and bowel disease. You might find them in coconut milk and almond milk.

Non-Organic Wheat, Corn, and Oats

Associated with pesticides

Sodium Acid Pyrophosphate

Associated with chemicals

Sodium Benzoate

A preservative

Soy, Soy Protein, Soya, Soba, Yuba, Soy Vegetable Protein, Mono-Diglyceride, Protein Isolate

These are highly refined. There are concerns that consuming larger quantities of these legumes and/or ingredients can block nutrients in the body. In the United States, soybeans are most frequently made with GMOs. (See GMO info above.)

Wheat Flour, Unbleached Wheat Flour, Unbleached Enriched White Flour, Unbleached Unbromated Wheat Flour

These are highly processed and don't help slow blood sugar spikes

White Rice

Highly processed with low nutritional value. Organic brown rice is a better option.

Appendix D

Sneaky Sugars

These ingredients don't always include the word *sugar*, but they are sugar just the same:

agave nectar

Barbados sugar

barley malt

beet sugar

brown sugar

buttered syrup

cane juice

cane juice crystals

cane sugar

caramel

carob syrup

castor sugar

confectioner's sugar

corn syrup (and solids)

crystalline fructose

date sugar

dehydrated cane juice

demerara sugar

dextran

dextrose

diastatic malt

diastase

ethyl maltol

evaporated cane juice

Florida crystals cane juice

free-flowing brown sugars

fructose

fruit juice

galactose

glucose

golden syrup raw sugar

grape sugar

honey

high fructose corn syrup

icing sugar

invert sugar

lactose (sugar in milk)

malt syrup (or dry)

maltodextrin

maltose

mannitol

maple syrup

molasses (blackstrap)

muscovado

panocha

powdered sugar

raw sugar

refiner's syrup

saccharine

sorbitol

sorghum syrup

sucrose

trehalose

turbinado

yellow sugar[69,70]

Notes:

- Although honey and maple syrup are sugars, raw honey and pure maple syrup are minimally processed, and they include phenolic content, like blueberries. They are also anti-inflammatory and antibacterial and have a lower glycemic index than other sugars (meaning they minimize sugar spikes), making them better choices than many other sugars.
- Some of the most damaging sugars (highly processed and high in glycemic index) on this list are maltodextrin, maltose, dextrose, and glucose.

Appendix E

Acid-and Alkaline-Forming Foods

A brief look at some acid-forming and alkaline-forming foods:[71]

Acid-forming foods

all meats

fish

poultry

eggs

margarine

most commercial cheese

pasteurized milk

most processed grain

pastas

crackers

noodles

refined sugar

pastries and candies

most nuts and seed

peanut butter

lentils

most legumes

soft drinks

coffee

commercial teas

most alcoholic beverages

ice cream

chocolate and cocoa

tobacco

NutraSweet, Equal, Sweet 'N Low

most prescription drugs

Alkaline-forming foods

most raw vegetables

most ripe, raw fruits

sprouts

sprouted whole grains

wheatgrass

sauerkraut

olive oil

goat cheese

raw milk

honey

molasses

maple syrup

apple cider vinegar

algae and sea vegetables

miso

soy sauce

Stevia

spices

herbs and herbal teas

green teas

Almost neutral (slightly alkaline-forming) foods

almonds

buckwheat

butter

millet

soured dairy products (yogurt)

Appendix F

Recommended Resources

Books

Adams, Patch, MD, with Maureen Mylander. *Gesundheit! Bringing Good Health to You, the Medical System, and Society Through Physical Service, Complementary Therapies, Humor, and Joy.* Rochester, Vermont: Healing Arts Press, 1998.

Gaynor, Mitchell L., MD. *The Healing Power of Sound: Recovery from Life-Threatening Illness Using Sound, Voice, and Music.* Boulder, CO: Shambhala, 2002.

Lipton, Bruce H., PhD. *The Biology of Belief: Unleashing the Power of Consciousness, Matter, and Miracles.* Carlsbad, CA: Hay House, 2016.

Meyer, Joyce. *The Everyday Life Bible: The Power of God's Word for Everyday Living.* New York: Faith Words, 2006.

Ortner, Nicolas. *The Tapping Solution for Manifesting Your Greatest Self.* Carlsbad, CA: Hay House, 2019.

Perlmutter, David, MD, with Kristin Loberg. *The Grain Brain Whole Life Plan: Boost Brain Performance, Lose Weight, and Achieve Optimal Health.* New York: Little, Brown and Co., 2016.

Rosenthal, Elizabeth. *An American Sickness: How Healthcare Became Big Business and How You Can Take It Back.* New York: Penguin Press, 2018.

Sims, Alec W., and Jonathan Goldman. *Sound Healing for Beginners: Using Vibration to Harmonize Your Health and Wellness.* Woodbury, MN: Llewellyn Publications, 2015.

Tolle, Eckhart. *The Power of Now: A Guide to Spiritual Enlightenment.* Novato, CA: New World Library, 2010.

Turner, Kelly A., PhD. *Radical Remission: Surviving Cancer Against All Odds.* New York: Harper Collins, 2014.

Weil, Andrew, MD. *Spontaneous Healing: How to Discover and Embrace Your Body's Natural Ability to Maintain and Heal Itself.* New York: Ballantine Books, 2011.

White, Linda B., MD, and Steven Foster. *The Herbal Drugstore: The Best Natural Alternatives to Over-the-Counter and Prescription Medicines.* Emmaus, PA: Rodale, 2000.

Recipe Books

Beliveau, Richard, PhD, and Denis Gingras, PhD. *Foods to Fight Cancer: Essential Foods to Help Prevent Cancer.* London: DK Publishing, 2007.

Carr, Kris, with Chad Charno. *Crazy Sexy Kitchen: 150 Plant-Empowered Recipes to Ignite a Mouthwatering Revolution.* Carlsbad, CA: Hay House, Inc., 2012.

Ramke, Annette, and Kendall Scott. *Kicking Cancer in the Kitchen: The Girlfriend's Cookbook and Guide to Using Real Food to Fight Cancer.* Philadelphia: Running Press, 2012.

Uliana, Sophie. *The Gorgeously Green Diet: How to Live Lean and Green.* New York: Penguin, 2009.

Weber, Louis. *Foods That Heal,* Morton Grove, IL: Publication International, 2018.

Cancer Support Program

HealingStrong. https://www.HealingStrong.org.

The mission of HealingStrong is to connect, support and educate individuals facing cancer and other diseases through strategies that help to rebuild the body, retore the soul and renew the spirit. HealingStrong Groups can be found throughout the United States, Canada and several other countries.

Magazines

Clean Eating Magazine. https://www.cleaneatingmag.com.

CDs

Bodhipaksa. *The Wisdom of the Breath.* Louisville, CO: Sounds True, 2009.

Myss, Caroline. *Why People Don't Heal and How They Can.* Boulder, CO: Sounds True, 1997.

Naparstek, Belleruth. *A Guided Meditation for Relaxation and Wellness.* Health Journeys, 2001.

Tolle, Eckart. *What Is Meditation?* Eckhart Teachings, 2004.

Weil, Andrew, MD. *Breathing: The Master Key to Self Healing.* Boulder, CO: Sounds True, 1999.

DVDs

SFQ-Level One for Health with Master Chunyi Lin. Spring Forest, 2000.

The Epitome of Hyperbole by Brian Regan. Comedy Partners, 2008, and Paramount Pictures, 2008. (Comedian)

Acknowledgments

When I decided to write this book so many years ago, I had no idea how much would be required. I now believe it was by design that I didn't know, as it is entirely possible that I wouldn't have tried to follow this dream otherwise. But what always drove me through this self-imposed challenge was the idea that if just one person could benefit from just one thing in this book, it would be worth it.

As the book evolved, I began to realize that many people, not just one, could read this book, hear the stories, imagine themselves in them, and become inspired fighters for healing. In this way, *you* drove me beyond what I thought I could do. *You* were the driving force—and always have been. Thank you.

As grateful as I am to have the book in print, I am poignantly aware of the people in my life who helped me make this possible. First, I acknowledge my husband, Chuck, and daughters, Katy and Ellie, as my greatest inspiration in fighting my battle with cancer. How your love, belief in me, and support sustained me, you will never know. You all are truly the light of my life in every way, and I love you so much.

Much love to you, Mom and Dad, Jamie, and Karen. I am grateful for how you have always been there for me. Thank you for all of your support regarding the trials of my illness and for believing in me then and now.

Pam, thank you for always looking out for me and being such a dear friend. What a blessing you are in my life.

John and Tiffany, thank you for your grace.

Dr. Don Martin, retired senior minister of Alpharetta Methodist Church, I am thankful for your kindness, your support, and the way you gently helped me connect the dots in finding God without scaring me! Your humor and simple way of teaching this perfect love are gifts I will always carry in my heart and spirit. I will share it with others where I can.

Thank you, Adele Wang, for your skill and wisdom in supporting and teaching me what was possible. You are a gifted healer and visionary.

Blessings to Christine Gustafson, now with God beyond this realm, the first MD who believed in me when I said I believed I could beat it. You said, "I believe it too." I carry your grace with me still.

Dr. Mickey, MD, thank you for being an extraordinary surgeon and person. I am so grateful.

Dr. Bill Bannister, MD, and Shelby Marshall, we were right: God is all over this. Thank you both for being with Chuck and me at our darkest moment and sticking with us. We will never forget it.

Thank you, Dr. Jonas, for being with me from the beginning, hanging in there with me, and being patient with my many questions!

I am thankful for Dr. Chris Greene and Dr. Nelson Bulmash for teaching me about supplements and healing. Dr. Bulmash, thank you for cheering me on all the way with my audacious idea of writing this book.

Thank you, Phil Breakwell and Phil Kobierowski—you are my champions!

Valerie Rapowitz, thank you for your patience and kindness while helping me rebuild what was lost.

Diane Eaton, I appreciate your deft editing, knowledge, and clarity. Thanks for taking me on.

With deep appreciation, I thank my friends and family for reviewing this manuscript with your unique perspective and eye for detail: Karen Davidsen, Chuck Dickenson, Ellie Dickenson, Katy Dickenson, Greg Griffith, Jim Laguzza, Holly McCormick, Jennifer Schere, Tom Wunderle, and Pam Zeman. The book is better for it.

Extra thanks to Chuck for taking the brunt of my home editing requests on the fly, even during football season! Thank you for your steadfast patience and unwavering support of me in this process. You are one of the finest men I know—and my love forever.

And thank you to so many other people along the way who

encouraged me to keep working hard to get the book finished, saying, "I need your book! The world needs your book! Hurry up!"

Well, here it is.

Lastly and most ardently, I thank my loving God, Jesus, and my dear angels who led me to wellness and continue to stay with me in the boat we ride on this earth. My gratitude to you is immense—but you know that already.

Endnotes

Chapter 2: Key Concepts: How We Can Heal

1   Patrick Fagan, "The Effect of Pornography on Individuals, Marriages, Family, and Community," *Marri* (December 2009), https://downloads.frc.org/EF/EF12D43.pdf.
2   Cleveland Clinic, "Stress," updated February 5, 2015. https://my.clevelandclinic.org/health/articles/11874-stress.
3   Elizabeth Rosenthal, *An American Sickness: How Healthcare Became Big Business and How You Can Take It Back* (New York: Penguin Press, 2018).
4   Rosenthal, *An American Sickness*, 8.
5   Mitchell L. Gaynor, *The Healing Power of Sound: Recovery from Life-Threatening Illness Using Sound, Voice, and Music* (Boulder, CO: Shambhala, 2002), 8–9.
6   Gaynor, *The Healing Power of Sound*, 4.
7   Andrew Weil, *Spontaneous Healing: How to Discover and Enhance Your Body's Natural Ability to Maintain and Heal Itself* (New York: Ballantine Books, 1995), 64.
8   Weil, *Spontaneous Healing*, 64.
9   Weil, 65.
10   Weil, 314–315.
11   Kris Gunnars, "10 Proven Health Benefits of Turmeric and Curcumin," *Healthline* (July 13, 2018), https://www.healthline.com/nutrition/top-10-evidence-based-health-benefits-of-turmeric.
12   Linda B. White, Steven Foster, and the staff of Herbs for Health, *The Herbal Drugstore: The Best Natural Alternatives to Over-the-Counter and Prescription Medicines* (Pennsylvania: Rodale Inc.: 2000), 574.
13   Guido Shoba, et. al., "Influence of Piperine on the Pharmacokinetics of Curcumin in Animal and Human Volunteers," *Planta Medica* 64.4 (May 1998): 353–56, https://www.ncbi.nlm.nih.gov/pubmed/9619120.

Chapter 3: The Body: 9-1-1

14   Tanya Harter Pierce, *Outsmart Your Cancer: Alternative Non-Toxic Treatments that Work,* 2nd ed. (Nevada: Thoughtworks Publishing: 2009), 323.

15 Mitchell L. Gaynor, *The Healing Power of Sound: Recovery from Life-Threatening Illness Using Sound, Voice, and Music* (Boulder, CO: Shambhala, 2002), 60.

16 Kelly Bulkeley, "Why Sleep Deprivation Is Torture," *Psychology Today* (December 15, 2014), http://www.psychologytoday.com/us/blog/dreaming-in-the-digital-age/201412/why-sleep-deprivation-is-torture.

17 Eric Suni, "Teens and Sleep," *Sleep Foundation*, updated August 5, 2020, http://www.sleepfoundation.org/articles/teens-and-sleep.

18 National Institutes of Health (NIH) in partnership with National Geographic Channel and the Public Good Project, *Sleepless in America*, first aired November 30, 2014.

19 Mark Michaud, "To Sleep, Perchance to Clean," *Rochester Review* (January-February 2013): 15.

20 Jim Otis, *Sleep Well—Heal Well*™, through the Brain Time® Program, https://braintime.com.

21 NIH, *Sleepless in America*.

22 Otis, *Sleep Well—Heal Well*.

23 NIH.

24 Otis.

25 NIH.

26 Otis.

27 Andrew Weil, *Spontaneous Healing: How to Discover and Enhance Your Body's Natural Ability to Maintain and Heal Itself* (New York: Ballantine Books, 1995), 240.

28 Kelly Turner, *Radical Remission: Surviving Cancer Against All Odds* (New York: Harper Collins, 2014), 28.

29 Lise N. Alschuler and Karolyn A. Gazella, *Five to Thrive: Your Cutting-Edge Cancer Prevention Plan* (El Segundo, CA: Active Interest Media, 2011), 85.

30 Turner, *Radical Remission*, 28.

31 Turner.

32 Alschuler and Gazella, *Five to Thrive*, 140.

33 Weil, *Spontaneous Healing*, 200.

Chapter 4: More About the Body

34 Cheryl D. Fryar, Margaret D. Carroll, Joseph Afful, "Prevalence of Overweight, Obesity, and Severe Obesity Among Adults Aged 20 and Over: United States, 1960-1962 Through 2017-2018," *National Center for Health Statistics (NCHS)* (January 29, 2021), https://www.cdc.gov/nchs/data/hestat/obesity-adult-17-18/obesity-adult.htm.

35   Roberto A. Ferdman, "Where People Around the World Eat the Most Sugar and Fat," *The Washington Post* (February 5, 2015), https://www.washingtonpost.com/news/wonk/wp/2015/02/05/where-people-around-the-world-eat-the-most-sugar-and-fat.

36   Fryar, Carroll, Afful, *Prevalence of Overweight, Obesity, and Severe Obesity Among Adults Aged 20 and Over: United States, 1960-1962 Through 2017-2018.*

37   Tanya Harter Pierce, *Outsmart Your Cancer: Alternative Non-Toxic Treatments that Work,* 2nd ed. (Nevada: Thoughtworks Publishing: 2009), 315.

38   Pierce, 324.

39   Pierce, 329.

40   Pierce, 329.

41   B. J. Hardick, "The History of Detox—and Why It's Not a Fad," Drhardick.com, May 11, 2016, https://www.drhardick.com/history-of-detox. (*Be careful to use entire site as shown, including the period at the end*).

42   International Agency for Research on Cancer/World Health Organization (WHO), "IARC Classifies Radiofrequency Electromagnetic Fields as Possibly Carcinogenic to Humans," press release no. 208, May 31, 2011.

43   WHO, "Electromagnetic Field and Public Health: Mobile Phones," October 8, 2014, https://www.who.int/news-room/fact-sheets/detail/electromagnetic-fields-and-public-health-mobile-phones.

Chapter 5: The Mind: Moving Energy to Heal

44   Mitchell L. Gaynor, *The Healing Power of Sound: Recovery from Life-Threatening Illness Using Sound, Voice, and Music* (Boulder, CO: Shambhala, 2002), 86.

45   Belleruth Naparstek, "Meditation to Relieve Stress." CD-ROM (Health Journeys, 1995.)

46   Aldo Civico. "Champion Novak Djokovic Reveals the Power of Visualization," *Psychology Today* (September 17, 2005), https://www.psychologytoday.com/us/blog/turning-point/201509/champion-novak-djokovic-reveals-the-power-visualization.

47   Clifford N. Lazarus, "Can Visualization Techniques Treat Serious Disease?" *Psychology Today* (January 26, 2016), https://www.psychologytoday.com/us/blog/think-well/201601/can-visualization-techniques-treat-serious-diseases.

48   Gaynor, *The Healing Power of Sound,* 80–82.

49   American Music Therapy Association (AMTA), www.musictherapy.org.

50   Gaynor, 83.

51 *Alice in Wonderland* (film), directed by Tim Burton from a screenplay by Linda Woolverton, Walt Disney Studios: 2010. Based on *Alice's Adventures in Wonderland* and *Through the Looking Glass* by Lewis Carroll.

52 Kelly Turner, *Radical Remission: Surviving Cancer Against All Odds* (New York: Harper Collins, 2014), 176.

53 Jim Robbins. "Ecopsychology: How Immersion in Nature Benefits Your Health," e360.yale.edu (January 9, 2020), https://www.e360.yale.edu/features/ecopsychology-how-immersion-in-nature-benefits-your-health.

54 Kevin Loria, "Being Outside Can Improve Memory, Fight Depression, and Lower Blood Pressure—Here Are 12 Science-Backed Reasons to Spend More Time Outdoors," *Business Insider* (April 22, 2018), http://www.businessinsider.com.

55 Seong-Hyun Park and Richard H. Mattson, "Therapeutic Influences of Plants in Hospital Rooms on Surgical Recovery," *American Society for Horticultural Science* 44:1 (February 2009), http://doi.org/10.21273/HORTSCI.44.1.102.

56 Debra Rose Wilson and Eleesha Lockett, "Grounding: Exploring Earthing Science and the Benefits Behind It," *Healthline* (August 30, 2019), http://www.healthline.com/healthy/grounding

Chapter 6: The Spirit: Going Deeper

57 Eckhart Tolle, *The Power of Now: A Guide to Spiritual Enlightenment* (Novato, CA: New World Library), 104.

58 Tolle, *The Power of Now*, 218–19.

59 Tolle, 219.

60 Mary C. Neal, *To Heaven and Back: A Doctor's Extraordinary Account of Her Death, Heaven, Angels, and Life Again* (Colorado Springs: WaterBrook Press, 2012), 165.

61 Neal, *To Heaven and Back*, 206.

62 Michael A. Singer, *The Untethered Soul: The Journey Beyond Yourself* (Oakland, CA: Harbinger, 2007), 180.

63 Anita Moorjani, *Dying to Be Me: My Journey From Cancer, to Near Death, to True Healing* (Carlsbad, CA: Hay House, 2012), 68.

64 Moorjani, *Dying to Be Me*, 69.

65 Moorjani.

66 Moorjani, 69–70.

Appendix C: Food Additives to Avoid

67   Sophie Uliano, *The Gorgeously Green Diet: How to Live Lean and Green* (New York: Penguin, 2009), 132–35.

68   Jonny Bowden. "GMO Foods: It's What We Don't Know That Matters," *Clean Eating*, January 6, 2016; updated May 31, 2017, https://www.cleaneatingmag. com/clean-diet/food-health-news/gmo-foods-its-what-we-dont-know-that-matters/.

Appendix D: Sneaky Sugars

69   Lisa Richards, "56 Names for Sugar: Are You Eating More than You Realize?" *The Candida Diet* (October 19, 2014), updated October 24, 2018, https://www. thecandidadiet.com/56-names-sugar-eating-realize/.

70   Robin Hilmantel, "56 Different Names for Sugar," *Women's Health* (November 3, 2014), https://www.womenshealthmag.com/food/a19981764/different-names-for-sugar/.

Appendix E: Acid- and Alkaline-Forming Foods

71   Tanya Harter Pierce, *Outsmart Your Cancer: Alternative Non-Toxic Treatments that Work,* 2nd ed. (Nevada: Thoughtworks Publishing: 2009), 319–20.

About the Author

Jennifer Dickenson is an author, cancer survivor and wellness advocate. Through her experience fighting brain cancer (glioblastoma) she discovered many healing tools that she now shares with others.

At the time of her diagnosis, she was an experienced transactional lawyer and popular public speaker. Now, motivated by what she learned through her health journey, she speaks to others about healing, mindfulness, and spiritual growth.

A refreshing voice willing to think differently about healing, Jennifer inspires others with her story and the tools she teaches, reminding us that we are built to heal. Born and raised in New York, Jennifer now calls Georgia home with her husband and two daughters.

Website:www.JenniferDickenson.com

Printed in the United States
by Baker & Taylor Publisher Services